By the Sweat of Your Brow

Reflections on Work and the
Workplace in Classic Jewish Thought

By the Sweat of Your Brow

Reflections on Work and the Workplace in Classic Jewish Thought

by

David J. Schnall

The Michael Scharf Publication Trust of
Yeshiva University Press

Copyright© 2001
Yeshiva University Press

Library of Congress Cataloging-in-Publication Data

Schnall, David J.
  By the sweat of your brow : reflections on work and the workplace in Jewish thought /
  by David J. Schnall.
    p. cm.
    Includes bibliographical references and index.
    ISBN 0-88125-751-6
    1. Work—Religious aspects--Judaism. 2. Working class in rabbinical literature. 3.
  Work--Moral and ethical aspects. 4. Industrial relations--Moral and ethical aspects. 5.
  Labor laws and legislation (Jewish law) I. Title.

BM509.L2 S36 2001
296.3'83--dc21

                                                                    2001029397

Distributed by
Ktav Publishing House, Inc.
900 Jefferson Street
Hoboken, NJ 07030
201-963-9524 FAX 201-963-0102
Website www.ktav.com
Email: orders@ktav.com

Table of Contents

v

Acknowledgments

In any effort of this type there are countless individuals who contribute time and effort, whether direct or indirect, from the first conceptualization to the finished product. It is impossible to acknowledge all to whom thanks are due. Invariably some are omitted. I begin, therefore, by apologizing in advance, even as I express my gratitude to all those who shared of their wisdom and their insight during the course of my research, and who made contributions both substantive and stylistic. Needless to say, I take full responsibility for any errors found within.

There are several persons, however, who provided particular encouragement, personal and professional, in the planning and in the completion of this work. First is Dr. Norman Lamm, the president of Yeshiva University, and, I am proud to say, a family member, mentor, and good friend. Both by support and example, Dr. Lamm has created an academic environment in which Jewish tradition and creative scholarship are nurtured and valued. While he enjoys a well-deserved reputation as an eminent scholar and Jewish leader, he is also an individual of great warmth, understanding, and humanity.

My thanks also go to Dr. Sheldon Gelman, dean of the Wurzweiler School of Social Work and associate academic vice-president. A wise administrator, Dr. Gelman has always set high standards for his faculty, even as he provides them with the resources and the atmosphere to excel. I have gained much from our close working relationship over the past years, and for his consistent support I remain in his debt.

I also am indebted to the J. William Fulbright Foundation, under whose auspices I was able to pursue a sabbatical year in Israel as visiting professor and senior scholar at the Paul Baerwald School of Social Work of Hebrew University. Under the leadership of its dean, Professor Howard Litvin, I established close friendships with the distinguished members of its faculty, friendships that I hope will continue in the form of professional collaboration and personal collegiality in the years to come.

Recognition also must go to the many individuals who were instrumental in the review and revision of this book. This includes the editors of several journals who initially published the work from which some of the following chapters were derived: the *Torah U'Maadah Journal*, the *Orthodox Forum*, the *Journal of Jewish Communal Service*, the *Journal of Business Ethics*, and *Administration and Society*. In addition, several colleagues and institutions were instrumental in helping me shape and develop my ideas through a series of workshops and conferences over the course of my stay in Israel. These include Rabbi Chashi Friedman and the staff of the Van Leer Institute, Prof. Shmuel Sandler and the department of political science at Bar-Ilan University, and Rabbi Pinchas Rosenstein and the Center for Business Ethics at Machon Lev: The Jerusalem College of Technology.

At the same time recognition is due to the members of my immediate and extended family, all of whom were very much part of this enterprise. This includes Sima and Danny Weingarten, whose love and hospitality helped ease my time away, and Josh and Hudi Schnall for simply caring.

My in-laws, Rabbi Solomon and Mrs. Bertha Shoulson, have contributed much to my work through their love and concern, for almost three decades. Without them, this project might never have gotten off the ground. Gratitude goes as well to my children, Eliezer, whose comfort and convenience were held hostage to this work, and Etan and Yonina, who often made their way without me as the research and writing progressed.

No words can adequately express the immense debt I owe to my parents, Harry and Chani Schnall z"l, and the terrible gap I feel as a consequence of their loss. Their importance in my life has not waned, despite their absence. They have always been, and they continue to be, an inspiration for my efforts, personal and professional.

Finally, I express my love, admiration, and never-ending devotion to the one to whom this work is dedicated. Only she understands, and that is what makes it all worthwhile.

Preface

A student of political theory, conversant and comfortable with Western philosophical and ethical traditions while grounded intellectually and personally in the Jewish legal tradition, Professor David Schnall embodies the values that underpin the mission of Yeshiva University. In this recent work, *By the Sweat of Your Brow*, the author displays his affinity for, and commitment to, the teachings of Torah Umadda as he demonstrates his uncommon ability to move adroitly within both Jewish and general sources. He successfully explicates how our religious culture confronted and responded to the role of work and the workplace within the many diverse civilizations in which our people found themselves.

Looming large in his considerations is the understanding that both workers and employees are bound by a set of moral obligations that ultimately stem from the Sinaitic Revelation. Such "mutually-agreed to" belief patterns inform the special way Jews always approached labor negotiations throughout history. It is not too farfetched to suggest that, in modern and contemporary times, these Jewish attitudes, though expressed in different idioms, have served as a basis for conflict resolution in American industrial relationships.

Ever sensitive to the current Jewish communal scene, Professor Schnall is both analytical and heuristic when he explores the responsibilities and defines the limits that Jewish tradition places on those who work in Jewish leadership positions. Throughout Jewish history, one who toiled for the community was generously praised. Indeed, in recognition of what leaders give to their communities, the Jewish Tradition speaks clearly to issues of job security and even tenure. But, significantly, these leaders' powers were also controlled by a sense of public accountability and by the ethical parameters for public management established by the higher rule of the Torah. As with so many issues, Schnall sees and describes the elegant balances inherent in Jewish law and traditions.

It is quite evident from the range of his sources that it took considerable intellectual effort—much sweat from his brow—to produce *By the Sweat of Your Brow*. It is a consummate primer of Jewish worker-management relationships written by an expert who has, in fact, trained rabbis and communal officials in these values. Now, our author's uncommon skills and fine sensitivities are on display for a wider audience.

Norman Lamm
President,
Yeshiva University

To Tova,
My *Aishet Hayil*

"for you rise above them all"
(Proverbs 31:29)

1

Introduction

I

Attitudes toward work, the worker, and the workplace are an important facet of any religious tradition and systematic social culture. They encompass moral doctrines and social norms regarding both the centrality of work per se and the place of specific vocations and professions in the definition of status, success, and self-worth. This speaks to whether work is intrinsically valuable, morally enhancing, and good for the soul, and reflects on the nature of our employment and the compensation we receive as shorthand for our personal value and our contribution to society.

The sense and substance of these attitudes are rooted in deeply held values regarding human freedom, the dignity of the individual, and the organization of society. Similarly, religious traditions and social cultures provide us with a network of laws and customs that structure relationships between worker and employer. From this we may uncover the wisdom of a religion or culture regarding interpersonal ethics and the balance between the individual and the group relative to freedom of contract, personal accountability, responsibility for the other, and the role of the public authority to regulate them. The workplace becomes a microcosm of society. Along with

1

the family, the school, and the house of prayer, it serves as a primary agent by which the individual is socialized and trained in the norms of the culture and the community.

To be sure, sharp variations of ideology and practice are evident in all these arenas. For some cultures work is nothing less than evil, divinely decreed. Harsh and punitive, it was imposed upon humanity as a consequence of original sin. In others, work is intrinsically value-free, although it serves legitimate instrumental purposes as the tool through which one earns the amenities that make life bearable, including the leisure time in which to enjoy them. Still others look upon all forms of labor as the province of the slave, the peasant, and the ignorant brute. It is for them to labor so that philosophers and aristocrats can properly spend their time enjoying life's pleasures and indulging in exercises of the mind.

At the same time, physical labor has been raised to the level of religious obligation by which to glorify the Lord. Utilizing God-given skills and talents to help subdue the earth and make it flourish, one becomes nothing less than a partner in creation. By contrast, idleness is sinful and leads to still greater transgression, whereas the industrious prosper as a sign that they are among God's elect. Secular thought of this kind, especially the Marxist variety, identifies labor as the salvation of mankind otherwise alienated from the means of production. Such theories place the worker in the vanguard of society, but political leadership and social dogma fill much of the void that results from removing a deity from the formula.

Finally, work may also fill expressive needs, providing a personal identity and helping to place the individual within a properly ordered and structured society. In more recent reflections of this theme, the workplace is cast as a stage for individual growth and empowerment. It is the setting for personal fulfillment to which each laborer is naturally entitled. Here workers are expected to participate in the firm's economic and commercial decisions, and to play an important role in determining their own personal fate and that of the corporation.

Needless to say, such attitudes are inextricably linked to broader issues of individual autonomy, initiative, and control in a constellation of values that balance determinism with free will. How a culture defines work and workplace relations has much to do with its mix of optimism and pessimism, its faith in human mastery over a fate preordained by willful gods and the movement of constellations. Apart from their specific content, of course, the degree to which individuals subscribe to these values also plays an important role in their emergence as behaviors.

In the chapters that follow, we will attempt to summarize the primary attitudes and values of Jewish religious culture as it confronts and responds to the role of work and the workplace, and to their position in its view of the good society. We will consider the place of the worker in this scheme and the mutual obligations that tie worker and employer to a vision of ethics and morality ordained by the word of God. We will look at the peculiar bias of the Jewish tradition in favor of the laborer as a protected partner in this relationship, along with the special responsibilities of those who work for the public authority.

It should be noted that Jewish tradition knows two categories of employees. The first is the *kablan*, analogous to a self-employed and independent contractor operating on the basis of fee-for-service. The second is the *po'el*, closer to the full-time employee in a large industrial plant or private concern. Our emphasis will be on the latter as we seek a Jewish model for the work ethic and for workplace relations.

In so doing, we will consider *derush* and *mahshavah*, broad philosophic wisdom and theological speculation, alongside *pesak* and *hora'ah*, legal opinions and juridical decisions. In all cases, however, our intent is not to uncover binding and normative rulings, though doubtless they will emerge in the course of the discussion. Rather it is our hope to draw out the ethical and moral underpinnings of these speculations and opinions, to better understand what moves and drives them, and to place them on a rough comparative continuum with other cultural systems and religious traditions.

To pursue these objectives, we will plumb the literature of Jewish tradition, accumulated over a period of some four millennia, including:

- The Hebrew Bible and its classical commentaries.

- The talmudic text, along with the scholarly exposition built on it.

- The rulings of early Jewish authorities and their reasoning in response to specific cases and petitions brought before them.

- The codes and compendia of Jewish law and tradition, collected over the past fifteen centuries.

- Modern works that apply this tradition to emerging new economic structures and the technologies that support them.

Of course it should be understood that despite a serious attempt to cover as much of the relevant literature as possible, not everything could be included in equal thrust. Some of the chapters that follow—the discussion of the centrality of work, for example, or of the role of Torah study as a life's pursuit—naturally lend themselves more to moral and theological speculation than to legal reasoning. Others, such as the worker's right to organize or considerations of multiple employment, are by their nature more fully grounded in legal disposition.

In all events, we will try to balance fairly the mix of sources to be examined, never ignoring the philosophic and ethical reasoning that grounds the law, or the bottom-line implications of theology that give it currency. Yet it is inevitable that some sources will be underemphasized. In making these difficult choices, priority will be given to the normative and authoritative, *pesak* and *halakhah*, which is accorded the mainstream as precedent in Jewish thought, over *musar* and *derush*, that which is essentially philosophical or homiletic.

II

Such an ambitious exposition must be preceded by several caveats that provide an analytical context for the application of these sources to contemporary social and economic concerns. Jewish tradition provides bold contrasts in both time and place. Spanning some four millennia of recorded history over several continents and with numerous iterations of structure, institution, and context, it is a study in dislocation, diversity, and valiant attempts to maintain integrity and conformity in response. It incorporates legal code, case law, municipal regulation, and ethical standards for interpersonal and public behavior. While today its interpreters are found primarily in

Israel, the United States, and Western Europe, in times past they flourished within the disparate political systems of ancient Rome, Christian Europe, Moorish Spain, and the full expanse of the Arab world.

Its social, political, and legal culture developed in several overlapping phases. The earliest forms emerged while Jews were living as an independent national entity in their own land. Here an indigenous hierarchy emerged around a loose confederation of tribes led by local judges, military leaders, and prophets. Attempts to unify administrative and religious institutions followed. Religious worship and ritual were later centered in Jerusalem with the construction of a holy Temple organized and serviced by a complex system of priestly functionaries. This was complemented by a powerful though not uncontested monarchy often beset by internecine battles and civil strife. This structure underwent numerous revisions as the kingdom split into two independent political entities and involved itself in numerous foreign intrigues, revolutions, and alliances with larger and more aggressive regional powers.

Exiled from its land and robbed of its national identity in its later expressions, Jewish tradition was forced to seek continuity among host cultures whose hospitality varied from suspicious isolation to violent hostility. Still it retained control over the lives of its adherents through economic, religious, commercial, and social sanctions. These were supported by the absence of social alternatives outside the traditional structures, short of apostasy and conversion. Thus conformity was enforced when subtler patterns of socialization, group pressure, and religious inspiration proved insufficient. The result was a network of loosely aligned medieval communities stretching through Europe, the Mediterranean region, the Near East, and North Africa.

In the wake of the French Revolution and with the emergence of more amenable secular polities, notably in the United States and Western Europe, the power of these sanctions receded. With it, so did the control of classic culture, tradition, and community life. As emancipated citizens of liberal new commonwealths, Jews entered the general culture en masse. Though its control was narrowed as a result, the tradition was redirected, called upon to respond to contemporary challenges, particularly in the wake of the Holocaust and the national renaissance with the birth of modern Israel.

Aside from its chronology, Jewish tradition also exhibits several important characteristics that are partly a function of its unique historical circumstances. These are worth noting here in contrast with Western social culture, especially as manifested in the United States. The first concerns the role of freedom vs. obligation, of rights vs. responsibilities, in both personal relationships and public policy. American legal and political tradition places heavy emphasis upon individual rights, both enumerated and reserved, from freedom of speech to freedom of assembly, from the free press to the right to bear arms.

By contrast, the point of departure in Jewish thought is a complex of detailed and interlocking obligations, broadly and loosely dichotomized, which by inference and implication establish the rights of the other in the context of a mutually binding relationship. In one category stand ritual obligations that define theological and ecclesiastical relationships with the deity, and that bind Him as much as they do His creatures. In the second are included civil and interpersonal obligations that define and structure social responsibilities toward one's fellow, and by extension toward community, national culture, and simple humanity.

This network generates an organic, even corporate framework that establishes differentials of power and status as standards for valuation more than for privilege. In such a system, rights and freedoms are weighed against obligations, and it is not the individual that stands sovereign but the relationship. Thus, ownership that implies the liberty to willful and arbitrary action is replaced by custodial responsibility. Accountability is judged by the Lord in the celestial courts of the great hereafter, or by generations to come in the great tribunals of history whose rulings are grounded more in contribution to the public weal and the benefit of others than in acquisition and accumulation.[1]

Moreover, unlike American political culture, Jewish tradition venerates neither a struggle for freedom from executive and administrative power nor a "sovereign people," from whom a political or administrative elite derives the right to govern. Instead, at least in the ideal, executive authority and the rights of the governed each derive from and are limited by the word of God and those empowered to interpret it. The dignity of the individual is a function of his status as a servant of the Lord, for this means that everyone's ancestry and legitimacy are on the same plane of equality. The governed are not inferior to the governors. Like wealth and social status, administrative power imposes obligations more than freedoms.

Yet the least familiarity with Jewish history confirms that for tens of centuries, conditions were far less than ideal. Dislocation was an everyday factor as individuals and families were forced to flee their homes and seek safety elsewhere, even as whole communities were subjected to physical persecution or expelled outright. Therefore, while attempting to maintain the essential integrity of the tradition and its spirit, Jewish juridical development and public practice were pressed to accommodate capricious Gentile overlords, hostile religious authorities, and the violent passions of the local citizenry. A strategy emerged, following at least three related paths rooted in early sources but carefully elaborated over time.

The first was substantial license for local custom and usage to fill the breach when tradition was silent, and even to assume priority when strict adherence to tradition would cause undue hardship and make daily life untenable. This was applied mainly in the civil arena, in such areas as communal, financial, and social relations, but more than occasionally in respect to ritual and ecclesiastical concerns as well. Tolerance for local diversity became a powerful tool in confronting the unstable and insecure circumstances of medieval and modern Jewish life. It also allowed local communities to adopt the best practices and customs of their Gentile neighbors as models, bending and shaping them into acceptable and legitimate adjuncts to local Jewish tradition. While diversity often generated dissension and even bitter disagreement between communities, it was more than compensated by the allegiance and flexibility it afforded locally.

Second, and related to the first, though attempts at regional affiliation and administrative hierarchy met with occasional success, the locus of power in Jewish communal life was primarily municipal or local, especially in Europe. This lent an early "federalism" to Jewish communal administration.[2] It was a structure that fit neatly with the feudal societies within which Jewish communities found themselves, and, in part, it was shaped by that reality. Therefore, though it is appropriate to speak of tolerance for diversity between medieval Jewish communities in, say, Poland, Germany, or Morocco, adherence to local custom was enforced within these communities. Those who resided or did business there were expected to conform to local usage, absent stipulation or exemption, even in the face of scriptural or talmudic precedent to the contrary.

Finally, Jewish legal and political culture is characterized by a well-developed sense of dialectic. For virtually every position, there is an opposition, for most every proof-text, a counter-text—each grounded in deductive argumentation, homily, and precedent. This lends vibrancy to classic Jewish study and vitality to the tradition it has fostered over the ages. Dissenting and minority opinions are preserved for their intrinsic worth. Yet given the dislocations we have mentioned, these opinions are also venerated for their potential use as future precedent, should changing circumstances require normative reexamination. The result is a framework for change that affirms fluency with the past while accommodating slow and deliberate elasticity. For the most part, it has held in hostile and hospitable environs alike.

In this vein, the traditional study of Jewish text, along with the reasoning it engenders and the conclusions it supports, has a distinctly "ahistorical" bent. It favors the argument upon its merits, almost, though not quite, regardless of its context. It abuts the parties to a debate as if they were partners sharing a common bench in the study hall and poring over the same worn, dog-eared volume, preferring to ignore or de-emphasize the reality that separated them by hundreds of years and thousands of miles. Political, social, and historical factors contribute to its diversity. Yet these are generally relegated to the shadows, only occasionally highlighted as the basis for a legal opinion or as the driving force behind a communal ruling. This too fosters a sense of timelessness in the tradition. It helps tie not just its spirit, but also its details, to obscure and otherwise forgotten institutions of a time long past.[3]

III

But our intent in this work is to speak not only to those whose primary interest is the analysis of Jewish thought and practice, important as such an objective may be. We are committed to the idea that this area of organizational ethics and employee relations may provide important theoretical and practical insight to students of human resources and of economic policy, as well as to the supervisors and managers empowered to apply such insight.

In the realm of organizational theory, for example, Jewish values in the workplace may shed valuable light on the foundations of modern commercial and economic relationships. Religious traditions have long been noted for their simple wisdom and understanding in areas related to the human condition. While generally relegated to the realms of theology and social philosophy, it may require only a small leap of faith to apply such principles to the modern organization and to utilize them as models for management. All great religions are replete with ethical and theological mores. Yet it is their application to the routine and mundane needs of the faithful that is the arbiter of their success and their retention into the next generation. Here we confront one of the most mundane and yet vital of all socioeconomic environments: the workplace.

Further, to the extent that Western organizational forms emerge from the Judeo-Christian tradition, the norms and practices of classical Jewish thinkers and their followers elucidate contemporary usage. These customs, and the issues that arise around their specific use, speak volumes about the daily commercial and social life of their adherents, the antecedents of current entrepreneurs and managers. If nothing more, it may be consoling to learn that the problems faced by managers today are neither new nor peculiar to their circumstances. In fact, they were faced and adjudicated—with greater or lesser success—centuries earlier under very different circumstances and in disparate venues.

Additionally, much is currently being said about the polyglot nature of the contemporary organizational environment and the importance of sensitivity to the social and cultural context of its management. An analysis of Jewish parameters may help inform strategies for supervision and workplace relations. Similarly, numerous aspects of social policy are linked to cultural differences in attitudes toward work and the worker. The success of programs dealing with unemployment, particularly among the immigrant poor, requires an appreciation for differences in their priority of work over personal morality or family status in defining social worth. So, too, the scope and substance of preretirement counseling must often contend with culturally based assumptions regarding vocation, and with a disdain for idleness and unproductive behavior.

Aside from academic or philosophic considerations, these differences, the attitudes they spawn, and their translation into behavior have assumed increased practical importance in recent years. The international horizons of business are rapidly expanding as firms continue to open plants and installations far from their home bases, and become more dependent upon foreign suppliers for everything from new technologies to spare parts. By the same token, the fall of political barriers and obstacles over the past decades has witnessed a rapid increase in investment opportunities in areas with unfamiliar histories and traditions. This is matched by indigenous entrepreneurs searching for venture capital from a growing pool of international investors.

Advances in telecommunications and in computer technology have facilitated collaborative research and development over long distances with unprecedented ease. Under such circumstances, national and cultural variations in work ethic, employee relations, and the structure of the workplace play a vital role among those who comprise the local human resource base for multinational and cross-cultural initiatives. Understanding these variations may help managers and executives respond to basic differences in such concrete areas as punctuality, absenteeism, accuracy, or efficiency even as it helps them prepare effective policies regarding the more subtle concerns of job satisfaction, motivation, and corporate loyalty. Finally, it may serve collaborators in cross-national commercial enterprises or applied research to overcome conflicting work norms that hamper otherwise successful joint ventures.

Closer to home, the movement of large refugee and immigrant populations due to political unrest, social or religious intolerance, the search for economic mobility, or simple wanderlust has made a polyglot of many large Western industrial centers. Managers face a diverse workforce even as corporations discover increasing cultural variation within their managerial pool. Universities, hospitals, and other centers of research and technology also have spawned a mix of national and religious values in their professional staff. Capturing the work norms and the attitudes nurtured by this diversity becomes a crucial aspect of productivity, efficiency, and the effective provision of service.

Of course, Jewish tradition is no monolith. From talmudic times to the present, some have applied it strictly and some have read new ideas and values into text and precedent, some have been zealous in protecting private property and managerial prerogative and some more concerned with the needs of workers and their families. Those seeking clear direction for intricate modern concerns must generally satisfy themselves with discernible trends and parameters that mesh the social, the economic, and the ethical. Moreover, complex organization and corporate structure was not characteristic of early Jewish life. To extrapolate modern application, its principles must serve as a heuristic, spread across a broad organizational structure.

Nevertheless, much of value may be inferred from the principles and directions that Jewish tradition provides. Its flexibility and tolerance for diversity have been briefly presented already. They will be elaborated in the chapters that follow. We also will examine its call for balance between the mundane workaday world and a life of personal fulfillment and spiritual growth. We will consider its commitment to equity in the workplace, its demand for compassion and understanding in matters of liability and loss, and the obligation it imposes upon the worker for both quality and productivity. Each of these speaks clearly to the issues raised above and discussed in more depth in the course of this book.

1. See Robert Cover, "Obligation: A Jewish Jurisprudence of the Social Order," *Journal of Law and Religion* 5 (1987): 65–90; Aaron M. Schrieber, *Jewish Law and Decision-Making: A Study Through Time* (Philadelphia: Temple University Press, 1979); Shmuel Shilo, "On One Aspect of Law and Morals in Jewish Law: 'Lifnim Meshurat Hadin,'" *Israel Law Review* 13 (1978): 359–390.

2. See Daniel Elazar, "The Kehillah: From Its Beginnings to the End of the Modern Epoch," in *Comparative Jewish Politics: Public Life In Israel and the Diaspora*, ed. Sam Lehman-Wilzig and Bernard Susser (Jerusalem: Bar-Ilan University Press, 1981); also Daniel Elazar, *Kinship and Consent: The Jewish Political Tradition and Its Contemporary Uses* (Lanham, Md.: University Press of America, 1983); and idem,

The Jewish Polity: Jewish Political Organization from Biblical Times to the Present (Bloomington: Indiana University Press, 1985).

3. Suzanne L. Stone, "In Pursuit of the Counter Text: The Turn to the Jewish Legal Model in Contemporary American Legal Theory," *Harvard Law Review* 106, no. 4 (1993): 813–894; Steven Friedell, "The 'Different Voice' in Jewish Law: Some Parallels to a Feminist Jurisprudence," *Indiana Law Journal* 67 (1992): 915–949.

2

Legal and Conceptual Bases of Jewish Labor Law

I

Jewish tradition exhibits a keen appreciation for the imbalance that typically exists in social relationships. Especially in the financial and economic realm, it tilts in favor of those, absent privilege and prerogative, whose weakness may result in their abuse. These include obvious and well-known examples, such as the widow, the orphan, and the poor, whose demand upon our compassion is mandated by biblical writ. The tradition also bids us recall the needs of the renter, the consumer, the borrower, and the employee. In large measure this consideration grew from their tendency to be less affluent and to have fewer rights than their counterparts in the commercial equation. However, aside from their material or legal status, their position in a transaction was seen to put them at a disadvantage, and this merited the protection of both public authority and religious norms.

Yet the social goal pursued by the interpreters of the tradition was not equality per se, but rather moral reciprocity and

Portions of this chapter originally appeared as "Exploratory Notes on Employee Productivity and Accountability in Classic Jewish Sources," *Journal of Business Ethics* 11, no. 6 (1993): 29–35 balance. They never questioned the legitimacy of private property, nor were they indifferent to social disparities, whether ritual, political, or economic. To mandate a crude and abusive uniformity that undermined choice was unnatural, and in any case naive and unenforceable.

Instead, they sought to limit the discretion of ownership against countervailing claims of public interest and personal obligation, under the aegis of a moral code to which all parties must owe allegiance. The point was to fashion a relationship based on equity and fairness, with a vision rooted in the inherent dignity of all the parties to a transaction, bound to one another as servants of the Lord and as adherents to His creed.

This bias toward the weak and vulnerable in the context of social equity is hardly more evident than in the parameters forged in the relationship between workers and employers. The tradition operates on the assumption that laborers were needy, that their living was hand-to-mouth, and that they depended upon their daily wages to support their families and fill their immediate needs. For this reason alone the laborer "gave his very spirit" to the task, even taking undue risk and subjugating his freedom to the whim of another.

Yet the rabbis also understood that workers were often lazy and unmotivated. They would take unfair advantage of their employer's absence and exhibit behavior that could only be described as disloyal and insubordinate. Neither should one depend upon their enthusiasm for the task or their concern for the product and equipment under their care. Close supervision was the proactive rule alongside a detailed schedule for liability in cases of damage or loss, which were frequent.

Our intent in this chapter is to provide an overview of major legal and philosophical instruments employed in structuring a workplace to balance these concerns, the base from which they grew, and the values that they represent. In so doing we will consider:

- The biblical sources for the inherent freedom of the worker and the demands placed upon the employer.

- The expansion and elaboration of these sources through talmudic insight and a keen sense for the realities of the commercial environment, both within the Jewish community and in its contact with Gentile hosts.

- The role of prevailing market conditions and business practices as a presumed and unspoken clause to the labor contract, even if they run contrary to the demands of Jewish law and precedent.

- The responsibility of workers to serve in a diligent and competent fashion, always pursuing the best interest of their employers.

II

Among the concerns that drive Jewish labor legislation was the fear that the employment relationship might evolve into something akin to indenture. The classical rabbis acted to instill justice and compassion in the workplace, lest the employer, individual or corporate, become a master and the worker virtually enslaved to his job. To this end, they invoked a scriptural reference wrested from the context of indenture and servitude (Leviticus 25:55). As a reminder to both master and employer, the Bible declares that the children of Israel are servants of the Lord, who rescued them from their bondage in

Egypt. The Talmud expands the reference by adding that they are servants only to Him and to no other (Bava Metzia 10a).

To be sure, Scripture provides indenture as an option for those to whom abject poverty leaves no choice but to place themselves in servitude. It is also offered as a means of compensation for crimes against property (Exodus 21:2–6, Leviticus 25:39–43, Deuteronomy 15:12–18). Still, medieval authorities reasoned that freedom was the natural state for a people who were to be servants only to the Lord. No matter how dire the circumstances or how pure the motivation, an indentured Hebrew transgressed this most fundamental principle.

Indeed, talmudic sources make the point precisely, in reference to the practice of piercing the ear of a servant who chooses to remain with his master even past the expiration of his term (Exodus 25:1–6, Deuteronomy 15:16–17). Rabbi Yohanan ben Zakkai tells us that it is appropriate to so mark the ear of one who had heard the Lord command that the children of Israel were only to serve Him. That the ritual was performed before the doorposts of the home leads Rabbi Shimon to recall the Israelite slaves in Egypt. They were spared God's ultimate plague by painting their doorposts in blood so that they would be redeemed and serve Him alone. One who voluntarily rescinds his own freedom should bear a mark on his ear and stand witness before the doorposts as well (Kiddushin 22b; see also Tosefta Bava Kamma 7:2).

The commentaries even entertained the thought that this mandate to freedom might prohibit any form of labor subordinate to another. If one is to serve only God, they reasoned, if indenture whether from poverty or criminal prosecution transgresses His will, then perhaps one may never be beholden to another, even if he pays a wage in return. Along with freedom, therefore, self-employment is the natural human state. While an intriguing proposition, the consensus appears to be that proscriptions against indenture, which threatens the very integrity of the person, cannot be extended to employment, in which one remains inherently independent.[1]

However, given their concerns about his person, the rabbis strained to ensure that the worker retain his liberty in both fact and appearance by granting him important benefits and prerogatives. For example, symbolic of their freedom of action and movement, workers were free to rescind the terms of their employment, "even in midday." This was later curbed and bounded if there was clear loss or damage to the erstwhile employer who was obligated by their agreement. Of course, a worker was expected to refund any payment he had received for work left unfinished. However, if his funds were insufficient, he could carry the debt over time with no prejudice against his option to leave (Bava Kamma 116b, Bava Metzia 10a).[2]

Similarly Scripture refers to the efforts of the Hebrew servant as "double the hire" of a worker (Deuteronomy 15:18). Since the normal term for such a servant was six years, the life of an employment contract was often limited to three. Anything beyond that was looked upon as dangerously close to indenture, and might "enslave" the employee by its conditions. Consider this, from Rabbi Mordecai ben Hillel: "More than three years removes one from the category of a worker. Though he is not a servant in all its laws, since he has removed himself from the category of a worker, he has transgressed 'for the children of Israel are servants to Me.'"[3]

The image of indenture and the legal mandates that governed its status influenced the protection of employees in other important ways. There arose, for example, a predisposition to assure them of all the benefits and prerogatives due a Hebrew servant. If one who violates a fundamental religious principle by bartering away his freedom is still entitled to various personal and material considerations, the rabbis reasoned, certainly these also should accrue to those who find a more legitimate route to earn their livelihood.

The reasoning is succinctly stated in rulings issued by the medieval sage Rabbi Meir ben Baruch of Rothenburg. In his words: "All that is lenient for a Hebrew servant is extended to the laborer, a fortiori. For the Hebrew servant has transgressed, and nevertheless the Merciful One has been lenient. Therefore certainly a laborer who has not so transgressed has the same benefit."[4]

This thinking found ample expression in at least two areas of worker benefit: severance pay and sick leave. In the first instance, Scripture mandates that when the term of indenture expires, the master of a Hebrew servant must deal kindly and compassionately with his departing charge (Deuteronomy 15:12–15). He must share the best that his fields and his flocks produced during the years of the servant's tenure. Whether this was integral to his remuneration or grounded in philanthropic impulse, the master is adjured not to "let him go empty."

Though the practice of indenture was discontinued with the destruction of the Temple, here was a model for severance benefits to all types of employees. The most likely current analogue to the indentured Hebrew was the *po'el*, the full-time worker. As such, he was entitled to similar treatment, even if his tenure was substantially less than then the six-year term typical of Hebrew servants.[5]

Regarding sick leave, the Talmud tells us that a Hebrew slave may miss as many as half the days of his indenture, that is, three years, due to sickness or injury, without being liable for the time lost. At the expiration of his service he is free to leave, and he need not compensate his master for time lost (Kiddushin 17a). In a series of cases involving tutors hired privately by a family, medieval thinkers invoked the indentured servant as their model once more, arguing that the employee should be extended similar liberty, for "all that is lenient for a Hebrew servant is extended to the laborer."[6]

However, the authors of Tosafot took exception, true to their emphasis on the contrasts between the employee and the indentured servant. In addition to a series of arguments based largely on talmudic text, they reasoned that one controlling a Hebrew servant has title to all his efforts rather than to the completion of any specific service. Therefore, the master is also subject to the servant's limitations. Should he fall ill or be injured, therefore, the master can have no claim against him, nor can he defer the term of his indenture. With a yeoman employee, such as a tutor, however, it is his skill and competence that have been transacted, for an agreed period of service. If he fails to complete his commitment, he has no claim other than to be compensated for the work he actually performed.[7]

Apart from his freedom from indenture, it is appropriate to invoke yet another talmudic source that provides an analogous claim to the inherent dignity of the worker. It emerges from a workplace anecdote involving a sage who was also an employer, Rabbi Yohanan ben Massiya.

[He told his son:] "Go and hire workers for us." He went and arranged to provide meals for them. When he returned, his father said to him, "My son, even if you provide a meal fit for King Solomon himself, you will not have fulfilled your obligation, for they are the children of Abraham, Isaac, and Jacob.

Before the work has commenced, go and specify that we will provide only bread and beans."

(Bava Metzia 83a)

Beyond the extent of his responsibility to provide food on the job, a question that was later mooted by the Talmud itself, Rabbi Yohanan furnishes us with yet another principle basic to the Jewish image of workplace relations. Despite differences in their status, workers can point to at least one important bond in common with their employers, their distinguished lineage. Reinforcing their claim to serve the Lord alone, they also stem from the biblical patriarchs. They command respect and dignity from their employer on this basis as well, their lesser station notwithstanding. The point has its analogy in public leadership. Communal administrators and trustees are warned never to exhibit willful arrogance or to take their constituents lightly. If nothing else, they must be treated with reverence and respect as the worthy scions of illustrious ancestry.[8]

It should be noted that the tale of Rabbi Yohanan ben Massiya and his employees is applied elsewhere, regarding a complex discussion of the efficacy of verbal contracts (Bava Metzia 49a). There the Talmud takes exception to what appears to be an instance of an employer unilaterally vacating an unqualified agreement to provide food for his workers. The rabbis deflect the objection by explaining that the otherwise binding nature of this verbal contract was linked to the employees and their understanding of the employer's terms.

If the incident occurred before the employees began working, one might infer that they were not satisfied that the son had the authority to execute such a commitment and therefore were awaiting Rabbi Yohanan's approval. Since no contract had yet been consummated, the terms could still be revised.

However, if work had begun, this would have been a clear indication that they had accepted his son's authority as proxy for their employer, and Rabbi Yohanan would be bound by the terms transacted in his name. For our purposes, however, the dignity of his employees, based on their venerable pedigree, was never impugned.

III

Quite beyond the integrity of their persons, workers are due special consideration because of their presumptive need. Employers are expected to impart kindness and compassion above the prescriptions of the law's strict letter. According to many authorities, this stands as corollary to a broader legal principle known as *lifnim mi-shurat ha-din*, the moral and even legal injunction to extend oneself beyond the formal lines of the law. The application of this principle to workplace relationships is grounded in yet another talmudic anecdote (Bava Metzia 83a) with a parallel text in the Jerusalem Talmud (Bava Metzia 6:6), but the former is typically invoked in normative discussion.

The anecdote tells us that Rabbah bar Hanna (by some readings "bar Hanan" or "bar Rav Huna") engaged porters to move barrels of wine. In the process the barrels broke and he confiscated their clothing against his loss, an action specifically proscribed in regard to a debtor but not clearly prohibited in cases of damage. The porters petitioned Rav, presumably the presiding judicial authority. He ruled:

> "Return their cloaks."
> "Is that the law?" [asked Rabbah bar Hanna].
> He answered, "Yes, 'so that you walk the good road' (Proverbs 2:20). "

They [the porters] then said to him, "We are poor, we have
worked all day and we are hungry. Shall we get nothing?"
Said he [Rav], "Go and pay them."
"Is that the law?" [asked Rabbah bar Hanna].
"Yes," he answered, " 'and the paths of the righteous shall
you guard' (Proverbs 2:20)."

On its face, this incident stands as a powerful precedent,
mandating extra measures of compassion from employer to
worker. Whether by their negligence or purely by accident, the
porters had clearly caused a loss. About this there was no dispute. Rabbah, their employer, may have been well within his
rights to demand from them a surety against compensation,
which given their impoverished state, would have been long
in coming. Yet it appears that he is forced by law to return their
cloaks. Moreover, in consideration for their financial need, he
is required to compensate them for their time. Again, as presented in the text, when confronted directly, Rav, the presiding
justice, confirms that his ruling is rooted in neither personal
compassion nor charitable impulse. Rather, it is handed down
as legal directive.

Talmudic commentators and the authors of the classic codes
of Jewish law were much exercised by both the style and the
substance of this judgment. For some it was evident that action
standing above the line of the law is purely that, and no more.
It could not be imposed by the courts no matter how compelling the context or how needy the beneficiary. To be sure,
the most likely intent of the scriptural admonition against par-
tiality in judgment was to prevent bias in favor of the wealthy,
a common happenstance. Yet its language also warns against
an assertive judiciary that overreaches on behalf of the weak,
no matter how laudable and well intentioned its motives
(Exodus 23:3, Leviticus 19:15, Deuteronomy 16:19, 24:17).

Interlocutors argued that when, in its estimation, the claimant is financially able, the court may set aside such a judgment and find on behalf of a needy petitioner, even if the claimant is disadvantaged as a result, indeed even if the inclination of the law appears to the contrary. This fulfills the scriptural demands to reach beyond the letter of the law (Exodus 18:20, Deuteronomy 6:18), a practice to which even the Almighty is said to subscribe (Berakhot 7a, Avodah Zarah 4b). Precedent exists in related cases dealing with assisting the wayfarer (Bava Metzia 30b), with malpractice among expert consultants (Bava Kamma 99b–100a), and with the return of lost valuables (Bava Metzia 24b). It is reasonable to also apply the principle to the interests of poor workers.

Aside from these doctrinal differences, the commentaries debate some crucial details of the case. For many, the outcome turns on the question of negligence. Rabbah's porters were liable because the damage was caused by their insufficient care in transporting his goods. Else they could have acquitted themselves by accepting the special oath instituted for precisely such events. Indeed this is the talmudic context within which the case emerges.[9]

Others claim that the affair was nothing more than happenstance, a common accident quite typical in such enterprises. Yet the porters stand accountable for damages, nevertheless. By the strict letter of the law, a worker bears a responsibility for his employer's wares and equipment equal to that of a paid watchman (Bava Metzia 80b). Normally this would free him of liability in the case of an unforeseeable accident. What occurred here, however, while not negligent was preventable. The porters therefore must make compensation for the damage.[10]

Authoritative opinion is found on all sides of the issue. Some record it as normative, without noting whether the source is legal or purely moral in nature.[11] For others, the demands of compassion are sufficiently powerful to contravene liability for damage. Consequently, the employer can be compelled by law to act in a kind and charitable fashion, even foregoing a judgment to which he is entitled. In the far term, such lenience works to the benefit of employers. If workers were not protected and held blameless against damage, it would be most difficult to recruit anyone—porters, for example—to engage in high-risk occupations.[12]

By contrast, some readings of the text excise the words in the passage that suggest Rav's intent to read compassion as a basic part of the legal structure. In these versions, when asked whether this is indeed the law, he simply quotes the verse from Proverbs cited above, without elocuting assent. By implication, the entire discussion operates on a moral plane only. Indeed, the medieval authors of the major Jewish codes, Rabbi Moshe Maimonides, Rabbi Yaakov ben Asher, and Rabbi Yosef Caro, ignore the case. Though they deal with the matter of *lifnim mi-shurat ha-din* as a general legal principle, they do not include our text or its implications in their normative rulings.[13]

Following this theme, the troublesome anecdote has more recently been applied in a revised context, where the judicial decision was never intended to be binding.[14] This is precisely why Rav ignored the scriptural verses more commonly invoked in this regard and chose instead to cite a verse from the Book of Proverbs, not generally employed as a sourcebook for legal opinions. His intent was merely to illustrate a moral and ethical model to a learned colleague. While equality before the law may be a basic legal standard for most people, more is expected from one who styles himself a righteous scholar, democratic theory notwithstanding. At times, an illustrious station entitles one to benefits and exemptions, but at other times, it imposes special responsibilities to act in an exemplary fashion, above and beyond the normative bar of justice.

As an alternative, the relationship between judge and petitioners here may better be understood as one of master and disciple. The correct identification of the parties, therefore, should be Rav and his student, Rabbah bar Hanna, or perhaps Rava and either Rabbah bar Hanan or Rabbah bar Rav Huna, all contemporaries in a later generation of talmudic scholarship. In each case the latter was a student of the former. This removes the discussion from the arena of liability and legal compulsion, and refocuses it as a genuine difference of opinion between student and teacher over a correct ruling in Jewish practice. The debate was grounded in three fine points of labor legislation:

- Are workers responsible for damage to an employer's property that results from negligence on their part?

- Is there license for an employer-cum-creditor (i.e., one to whom workers owe compensation for such damages) to take their personal property as security?

- What are the parameters of the talmudic decision to allow employees to free themselves of liability for damages through oaths of innocence?

Finally, Rabbi Shelomoh Edels provides an ingenious approach to the proceedings. He argues that indeed there was negligence here but not on the side of the porters. At least in part, responsibility for the damages must fall to Rabbah, the employer, who demanded that his porters follow an unsafe and risky route in transit. The verse chosen as legal citation, "so that you walk the good road and the paths of the righteous shall you guard," was intended as metaphorical rebuke. To be held liable for damages, the judge was suggesting, the porters must be permitted to travel the safest path, that is, "the good road." Indeed, this too was the substance of an immediately preceding talmudic discussion. Rabbah had not been fastidious in this regard. He had not "guarded the righteous pathway," allowing them to transport his goods by the route that represented the least risk. In consequence, the judgment was against him.[15]

These complexities and nuances aside, the case of Rabbah and his porters stands as a powerful precedent and model for employee relations in Jewish practice. Whether from legal reasoning or moral and ethical sensibility, employers are called upon to deal charitably with workers. The tradition demands that employees be treated with lenience and understanding, especially when they suffer want. They may be due compensation for their time even if the employer has suffered loss and damage.

IV

Even as the tradition exhibits a bias in favor of workers, because of both their financial need and their disadvantage in workplace relations, talmudic and rabbinic authorities were candid in their observations about the typical shortcomings of workers. They noted a distinct tendency toward sloth that too frequently led to a less than acceptable commitment to the job. The talmudic sage Rabbi Yohanan, for example, warns that to squander a large inheritance one need only hire workers and permit them to do their jobs unsupervised.

The commentaries say that this refers to agricultural workers, in particular those who toil in the vineyards. Having little concern for their employer's loss, they allow their oxen to trample the fields, damaging both produce and equipment (Bava Metzia 29b). Rabbi Yehudah ben Shimon expresses a related sentiment. Reflecting on the assiduous productivity of the patriarch Jacob in the fields of Laban, Rabbi Yehudah tells us, "It is the way of the world that laborers work faithfully for their employers for two or three hours, but then become lazy in their toil (Bereshit Rabbah 70:20).

Out of concern for the effective use of employees' time, the rabbis curtailed certain religious activities so as to reduce the distractions of workers on the job. For example, they composed an abridged daily prayer and grace after meals to accommodate the demands of the workday. In addition, they limited the extent to which those on the job could participate in certain religious and communal functions (Talmud Bavli, Berakhot 45b–46a, Kiddushin 33a, Hullin 54b).[16]

Moreover, their concern was not merely for chronic cases of low productivity. Even occasional inefficiencies were treated sharply, assuming that they resulted from lapses in performance. Maimonides, for example, warned laborers to be careful never to " steal" from employers "by wasting a bit here and there and completing the day with trickery."[17] Extending this concern, others ruled that those who took personal time without the prior consent of management could be dismissed, penalized for their time off the job, and then held liable for the cost of their replacement. The extent and nature of the penalty would depend upon the type of loss suffered by the employer, the point at which the work stoppage occurred, and the availability of an alternative labor supply. Special exemptions were made for emergency circumstances, such as illness, death in the family, accidents, and the like. Here employers are generally required to pay for work done until such an unforeseen occurrence, but they need not compensate workers for time off the job even in an emergency.[18]

Dissenting opinions soften these judgments, however, with the earliest being the most liberal. They suggest that employees who because of an emergency must leave their posts without managerial consent should suffer no penalty at all. Rather, they are entitled to compensation for the full term of their contract, even if they are never able to return to work. Similarly, if pre-payment was made beforehand, employees need not refund their wages for time off due to an emergency. Others strike a middle ground. They claim that the financial penalty should depend upon the employee's good faith. If he returns to his post of his own volition after the emergency has passed, and completes the work or the hours for which he was engaged, then no penalty need be imposed. However, if the emergency occurs at the end of the contract period or if management suffered irretrievable loss for time off the job, it may not be possible to compensate for time lost, and employees will be liable for damage caused by their absence.[19]

Contemporary authors have reasoned, therefore, that management can hold employees financially liable in instances of underproductivity.[20] Of course, a legitimate number of sick or personal days without penalty may be included as part of the initial work agreement. Additionally, local usage and custom regarding sick-days, personal days, and vacation time can be invoked as the arbiter of practical judgment. Then management could not claim that time was being taken without its consent.

Short of dismissal for malfeasance, employees may be held liable for damage to materials or equipment under their care as well as for the poor quality of their product or service. Such damage may be actual loss due to employee negligence in executing responsibilities. Alternatively it may be the consequence of poor performance reflected in an inability to adhere to an explicit managerial request or in a departure from generally accepted standards of quality. The negligent employee may also be liable for opportunity costs, including clear and measurable profit that would have accrued had there been no damage, or had delivery been made in a timely fashion at usual standards of quality.[21]

Such liability inheres even in cases of accidental damage. For example, employees bear responsibility for theft, loss, and most instances of breakage to product or equipment. The operative principle suggests that though damage was not a direct result of employee negligence, particular care for product and equipment is implicit in the employment contract. Damage implies that the employee did not exhibit sufficient concern. At least one recent authority advises lenience in cases of minor accidental damage, absent of gross negligence.[22]

As noted above, necessary concessions were made to the realities of the labor market. For example: "One engaged to move barrels from one place to another and they break, the law requires that he pay . . . but the rabbis ruled that he only be required an oath of non-negligence. For if you require that he pay, then no one will hire himself to move barrels."[23]

No matter how equitable, parameters for complex commercial relations that ignore the simple realities of the labor market render any ethical system irrelevant. Worse, they encourage constituents to take other prescriptions lightly. At best, adherents give little more than lip service to their obligations, fulfilling their demands formally and superficially, with little regard for the spirit and the sense that the norms imply.

V

Given the balance they tried to strike between a natural bias in favor of the worker and the legitimate productivity concerns of his employer, it is not surprising that the rabbis placed strong emphasis on *minhag*. Thus long-standing general practice and social usage, often rooted in religious text or practice, stands as yet another source contributing to Jewish perspectives on employee relations. The custom and tradition may be global, it may be defined by geographic locale, or its parameters may reflect the bounds of an industry or an economic sector. To be sure, the impact of *minhag* as a legal category is not peculiar to employment issues or commercial activity. Prevailing custom is understood as normative in religious ritual and in family law, as well as in social regulation.

However, there is reason to believe that much of the classical Jewish attitude toward the importance and vitality of *minhag* was shaped by its commercial application. Unlike differences in prayer, dress, or diet, which were frequently intended to create insulation between the Jewish community and its Gentile neighbors, to ignore prevailing commercial usage would have made it impossible for Jews to survive under already difficult circumstances. Consequently, the rabbis more often stood firm in their ecclesiastical and ritual determinations but made special efforts to accommodate tradition to the commercial and economic circumstances that surrounded their communities. This, in turn, was grounded in precedent immediately relevant to our discussion.

Consider the following, from the earlier portion of the Mishnah cited above regarding Rabbi Yohanan and his hungry workers:

> One who hires laborers and demands that they rise early
> and work late, in a place where it is not the minhag, he may not
> force them. Where it is the minhag to provide food, he must
> provide food, to offer fruit refreshments, he must offer fruit
> refreshments. Everything [is measured] by the custom of the
> locality.
>
> (Bava Metzia 83a)

Indeed the mishnah goes on to explain that Rabbi Yohanan
need not have fretted about their culinary demands. As with
any other unstated detail of the contract, lunchtime cuisine
had only to conform to local custom and no more.

In a subsequent discussion, the Talmud presents specific
scriptural guidelines that define the workday, local practice
notwithstanding (Bava Metzia 83a). Citing biblical writ
(Psalms 104:22–23), the rabbis demonstrate that the typical
hours of employment should properly commence with the
first rays of the sun and continue until nightfall, allowing special considerations for Sabbath preparations on Friday after-
noon. Nevertheless, local custom supersedes such regulations.
Unless stated otherwise, employees may presume that the
terms of their hire will conform to local *minhag* rather than prescriptions of the psalmist.

In their account of the text, the authors of the Jerusalem
Talmud extend the import of *minhag* from a narrow question
of the working day to the vast scope of Jewish tradition and
practice. In a broad and sweeping opinion, they record that
"this [ruling of the Mishnah] informs us that *minhag* nullifies
the law" (Bava Metzia 7:1, 11a). Though marked by specific
bounds and limits, that which is designated as prevailing custom may take precedence over enacted legislation, rabbinic
ruling, and even, as in our case, scriptural mandate. At face
value, long-standing practice fully abrogates the law. It is,

minimally, a presumed but unstated clause to any agreement. Absent stipulation to the contrary, the parties are bound by its dictates.

Later authorities refined the concept, providing structure and scope to the definition of *minhag*, and detailing the process of its formulation and acceptance. For example, in some accounts, *minhag* was more than simply a matter of popular usage that became ingrained in the social or economic fabric over time. To become normative, a *minhag* had to be rooted in or claim support from the store of non-legal Jewish literature, usually poetic, mystical, or interpretive, though not talmudic.[24] Others demanded that it reflect a scriptural reference, though without specific mandate. Still others saw the formation of *minhag* as a straightforward function of social history, a reasonable practice that has withstood the test of time and to which early local leadership concurred. Consequently, provisions were made for customs and practices that were considered unreasonable, grossly inequitable, or unfair. [25]

Just as workers ought not to be enslaved or indentured by the conditions of their employment, however, neither should they be harshly limited and restricted by prevailing practice. Within broad limits, the parties to a contract may voluntarily forego or ignore local custom, making separate agreements that nullify or modify its impact. This must be elocuted before witnesses or stipulated unambiguously in the contract. Absent such stipulation, an employer cannot normally claim, for example, that a higher wage is implicit evidence that personal expenses or compensation for a longer workday were understood and included, especially if prevailing practice is otherwise.[26]

As we will see in the chapters that follow, *minhag*, understood as prevailing business practice or local regulation, is a powerful tool in the process of elaborating contemporary employee relations. This includes retirement and severance benefits, unionization and the right to organize, job security, and occupational safety. As the circumstances of commerce and employment have changed over time, the flexibility of *minhag* has often been employed by religious thinkers to extend the interests of workers in areas not expressly provided or anticipated in classic Jewish thought. This has contributed to its elasticity and helps it serve as a viable basis for contemporary ethical discourse.

VI

In sum, attitudes toward the worker and the workplace flow from several disparate sources with roots not always peculiarly or uniformly Jewish. Those closest to the tradition emerge from the Bible directly. From Scripture, talmudic rabbis postulated that freedom was natural to the human condition and servitude reserved for the Lord alone. No matter how wealthy or how poor, no matter how distinguished or how demeaned, all members of the community were united by a bond derived from their common faith and ancestry.

Those who allowed their freedom to be curtailed, such as indentured servants or, according to preliminary analysis, even full-time employees, were guilty of sin. Yet there was no long-term recrimination. On the contrary, with the completion of their term of service, they were entitled to extra compassion and understanding, measured by the gifts they were due as they attempted to right their lives. This became a model for employees as well. Whether in the form of severance benefits, sick days, or simple understanding, they were to be treated no less well than their indentured counterparts.

This mix of legal formality and personal forebearance also emerges outside the model posed by Scripture, though it may be several steps removed from the core of the tradition. By some estimates it is implicit in biblical writ. Others allow it to be written into legal decision by sensitive and well-meaning jurists. Perhaps it is a mandated form of charity, and perhaps it is reserved only for the pious elite. Still, there is little question that the principle of *lifnim mi-shurat ha-din*, actions that are at once above the law and yet part of the law, is an important corrective for social or commercial imbalance. At the least, it stands as a heuristic from which the values of justice tempered by mercy may be implanted into the workplace. By its rule, judgments of liability may be set aside and wages paid to those who have been party to damage through but little fault of their own.

Yet employees are warned not to abuse their protected status. They are expected to care for their health, reserve their strength, and put their energies to the task. If they offer anything less, they are guilty of stealing from their employers. Save for emergencies, accidents, or other unforeseen circumstances, they will be held accountable for theft, loss, or damage to property and equipment. They also may be expected to compensate for any time lost. Their inherent freedom alongside their claim to compassion should not be understood as license for indolence, trickery, or sloth.

All this is reinforced by *minhag*, prevailing business practice, taking us far afield from what is peculiar or unique to Jewish tradition. Many of the advances that workers have experienced in the past century, in regard to occupational safety, educational benefits, or job security, were never anticipated in the traditional sources. Yet they have been incorporated into Jewish custom and practice, and enforced in binding arbitration or rabbinic ruling, as part of the prevailing *minhag*, customary business practice. The implications of so expansive a view of employee relations will be considered in the chapters that follow.

1. See, e.g., Tosafot Bava Metzia 10a, s.v. *ki li.*

2. See Rabbi Moshe Maimonides, *Yad ha-Hazakah*, Hilkhot Sekhirut 9:7; Rabbi Yosef Caro, *Shulhan Arukh*, Hoshen Mishpat 333:3.

3. Rabbi Mordecai ben Hillel, *Mordecai*, Bava Metzia 460.

4. Rabbi Meir ben Baruch of Rothenburg, *She'elot u-Teshuvot ha-Maharam mi-Routtenberg*, esp. 85 and 79; see also Rabbi Mordecai ben Hillel, *Mordecai*, Bava Metzia 347.

5. Rabbi Aharon Halevi, (?) *Sefer ha-Hinnukh* 483. There is some debate as to the authorship of this text hence the (?) following the name of the presumed writer.

6. Rabbi Mordecai ben Hillel, *Mordecai*, Bava Metzia 346; see also Rabbi Moshe Maimonides, *Yad*, Hilkhot Avadim 2:5.

7. Tosafot Kiddushin 17a, s.v. *hallah shalosh.*

8. See, e.g., Rabbi Moshe Maimonides, *Yad*, Hilkhot Sanhedrin 25:1–3.

9. See, e.g., Rashi, Bava Metzia 83a, s.v. *shkule.*

10. See, e.g., Rabbi Menahem Me'iri, *Beit ha-Behirah*, Bava Metzia 83a; also Rabbi Yosef Caro, *Shulhan Arukh*, Hoshen Mishpat 304:1.

11. Rabbi Asher ben Yehiel, *Kitzur Piskei ha-Rosh* 6:19.

12. Rabbi Mordecai ben Hillel, *Mordekhai*, Bava Metzia 257; also Rabbi Yoel Sirkes, *Bayit Hadash*, Hoshen Mishpat 12:4.

13. Rabbi Yosef Haviv, *Nimmukei Yosef*, Bava Metzia, p. 102. See also Rabbi Yaakov Ba'al ha-Turim, *Tur Shulhan Arukh*, Hoshen Mishpat 12:4. Also notable is the attempt by Rabbi Yehoshua Falk-Katz to read our case into the decisions of the *Shulhan Arukh*. See *Sefer Me'irat Einayim*, Hoshen Mishpat 304:1.

14. For a good review of this literature, see Shmuel Shilo, "On One Aspect of Law and Morals in Jewish Law: *Lifnim mi-Shurat ha-Din*," *Israel Law Review* 13 (1978): 359–390; Shillim Wahrhaftig, *Dinei Avodah be-Mishpat ha-Ivrri* 2: 924–928; Robert Eisen, "'Lifnim MiShurat Ha-Din' in Maimonides' *Mishneh Torah*," *Jewish Quarterly Review* 89, nos. 3–4 (1999): 291–317.

15. Rabbi Shmuel Edels, *Aggadot ha-Maharsha*, Bava Metzia 83a.

16. Rabbi Yaakov Ba'al ha-Turim, *Tur Shulhan Arukh*, Hoshen Mishpat 337:20; Rabbi Yosef Caro, *Shulhan Arukh*, Hoshen Mishpat 337:20.

17. Rabbi Moshe Maimonides, *Yad*, Hilkhot Sekhirut 13:7.

18. Rabbi Yaakov Ba'al ha-Turim, *Tur Shulhan Arukh*, Hoshen Mishpat 333:3; Rabbi Yosef Caro, *Shulhan Arukh*, Hoshen Mishpat 333:3.

19. Rabbi Mordechai ben Hillel, *Mordekhai*: Bava Metzia 346; Rabbi Meir ben Baruch, *She'elot u-Teshuvot ha-Maharam mi-Routtenberg* 85; Rabbi Yaakov Ba'al ha-Turim, *Tur Shulhan Arukh*, Hoshen Mishpat 333:3; Rabbi Moshe Isserles, Rema, *Shulhan Arukh*, Hoshen Mishpat 333:3.

20. Wahrhaftig, *Dinei Avodah be-Mishpat Ivri*, p. 324.

21. Rabbi Moshe Maimonides, *Yad*, Hilkhot Sekhirut 10:3–4; Rabbi Yaakov Ba'al ha-Turim, *Tur Shulhan Arukh*, Hoshen Mishpat 306:3; Wahrhaftig, *Dinei Avodah be-Mishpat Ivri*, pp. 814–816.

22. Rabbi Moshe Maimonides, *Yad*, Hilkhot Sekhirut 10:4; Rabbi Yosef Caro, *Shulhan Arukh*, Hoshen Mishpat 306:4; Rabbi Yehoshua Falk-Katz, *Sefer Me'irat Einayim*, Hoshen Mishpat 306:13; Rabbi Yehiel Mikhal Epstein, *Arukh ha-Shulhan*, Hoshen Mishpat, 331:7.

23. Rabbi Moses Maimonides, *Yad*, Hilkhot Sekhirut 3:2; See also Rabbi Yosef Caro, *Shulhan Arukh*, Hoshen Mishpat 304:1.

24. See, e.g., Rabbi Abraham Gombiner, *Magen Avraham*, Orah Hayyim 890:22; Rabbi Moshe Sofer, *She'elot u-Teshuvot Hatam Sofer*, Orah Hayyim 1:36.

25. Rabbi Mordechai Ben Hillel, *Mordekhai*, Bava Metzia 366; Rabbi Moshe Isserles, Hoshen Mishpat 331:1. Tosafot Bava Batra 2a, s.v. *bagvil*.

26. See, e.g., Tosafot Bava Metzia 83a, s.v. *ha-sakher*; Rabbi Arieh Leib *Ketzot ha-Hoshen*, Hoshen Mishpat 331:1.

3

The Jewish Work Ethic

I

No doubt the best-known and most enduring analysis of the link between religious culture and work values is Max Weber's seminal assessment of Protestant faith and the rise of capitalism.[1] In it, Weber argued that early Protestant religious thought, particularly the work of John Calvin, committed believers to a harsh, inescapable determinism. Here an unchanging God chooses those who will win grace and those who will be cursed, virtually at their birth. One could never be quite certain of his membership in the elect, the special group of individuals whom the Lord had chosen for eternal life, but outward testimony was available. Notably, financial success and personal prosperity would attest that the Lord had smiled upon one's fortune. These would best result from a single-minded commitment to a life of hard work and simplicity.

In many ways, Calvin was extending patterns already developed by Martin Luther, who argued that even the most menial work had dignity and religious significance. In reaction to the

---

This chapter and the one that follows are based on papers presented at the conference on "Jewish Ethics and the Workplace" at Bar-Ilan University, Ramat Gan, Israel, March 2000.

monasticism glorified during the Middle Ages, Luther claimed that it was for each individual to serve his ministry to God through his own vocation, which was a "calling." This boldly contrasted not only with medieval Christianity, but with earlier traditions.

For example, ancient Greek and Roman thought looked upon labor with disdain. Accumulated wealth was generally regarded as a means by which one might become independent and self-sufficient, an owner of property and free from toil. Manual labor was relegated to slaves so that free men might pursue warfare and commerce. [2]

Even among the free, status was apportioned not by how much work one did, but by how little. Those who toiled were looked askance. Their effort was redeemed only when it enabled members of the social elite to engage unfettered in philosophy, art, and politics. Nor was prosperity necessarily related to merit or personal virtue. Rather, moralists claimed that wealth was to be pursued for the good that might be performed with it.

Early Christian thinkers adapted many of these themes even as they introduced important shadings and nuances of their own. They affirmed that work was a punishment for original sin, an idea they had inherited from their readings of Hebrew Scripture. Gainful employment was valued only in that it averted dependence upon charity. Wealth created an opportunity to show gratitude to the Lord by sharing with the Church as well as with those less fortunate.

A life of reflection and contemplation was to be preferred over the toil and travail of the workaday world, although its focus was religious study and prayer rather than art or philosophic abstraction. Nonetheless, children were expected to continue in the vocations and pursuits of their parents, thereby ensuring the stability of the social structures God had ordained. This supported the emergent feudal order and retarded aspirations for economic mobility that might upset its growth.

In considering the impact of Protestant thought upon capitalist economics, Weber was particularly taken by certain ideas that were distinct and original to Calvin. For example, financial success and prosperity alone were not sufficient to mark one as a member of God's elect. Those chosen were also characterized by lives of disciplined austerity bordering on the ascetic. In this sense work was intrinsically valued on religious grounds, and not merely for the prosperity it might bring. Idleness and sloth were sinful, but so were materialism, opulence, and pride. One must work diligently, for an independent and industrious spirit paved the way to personal redemption. Beyond providing for basic personal needs, profit was not to be squandered on frivolous luxuries that marked the devil's temptation. Instead, it was to be reinvested so that it might yield still greater wealth and thus further testify to the righteousness of its possessor.

There was little point in providing assistance to those whose poverty and want suggested that they were not among the Lord's chosen. He had ordained that they would never raise their status. Instead, profits were to be reinvested in personal commercial ventures again and again, to amass wealth and thereby raise the economic well-being of the community at large. In fact by serving God through hard work and austere living, one became free of family tradition, and obliged to seek out those trades and professions that were the most profitable.[3]

Weber argued that these values promoted and encouraged radical changes in the economic system of Europe and later the New World. In his estimation, delayed material gratification created the pool of resources that was the basis for capitalist expansion. This in turn nourished more mobile financial systems which moved Europe away from the land-based economy that had reinforced feudalism and retarded growth.

Recent thinking has turned more materialist in reaction, suggesting that the causal power of the religious ideology emerging from the Protestant Reformation was a reflection and confirmation of other social changes already underway. Rapid population growth, especially in the big cities, inflation, high unemployment, and the discovery of the Americas conspired on their own to move European economic systems toward the modern structures of capitalism. The Reformation rode the coattails of these changes, providing a religious and philosophic framework for their expansion.[4]

Nonetheless, Weber insisted that the effects of the Protestant ethic could be observed and empirically measured. He argued that members of Protestant churches tended to work harder, save more, and show greater financial success than others, especially Catholics. He claimed that similar differences would be evident if one compared predominantly Protestant countries to those whose majority affiliated with other religions. Some writers have added that Protestant faith encouraged child-rearing practices that emphasized achievement and entrepreneurial success.[5]

Empirical attempts to examine Weber's propositions have followed two broad directions. The first employs a variety of measures generated to test the Protestant work ethic, including groundbreaking efforts to create a cultural taxonomy that considers:

- Masculinity—the value placed upon material success and assertiveness.
- Individualism—the value placed on personal interests over those of the group.

- Uncertainty—the value placed upon willingness to risk.
- Power distance—acceptance of unequal power distributions.

In this formulation, the Protestant work ethic stood at one pole of the continuum, with a strong emphasis upon the accumulation of wealth and the primacy of personal success, and a high tolerance for risk and for sharp social stratification as a natural (divine?) aspect of human organization. Various national cultures were judged, in large measure, by the degree to which they did or not confirm to these elements of Weber's Protestant work ethic.[6]

In addition, at least three popular scales have been developed to operationalize the Protestant work ethic as a personality variable. These provide a context for comparing it against social cultures that value work as a contribution to society ("organizational belief systems"), as a boon to individual growth ("humanistic ethos"), or as means to personal pleasure ("leisure ethic"). Finally, a major cross-national effort has explored the "meaning" of work, its centrality in the lives of respondents, its expected outcomes, and whether it is perceived as obligation or as entitlement.[7]

The results of these empirical tests are mixed, confirming Weber's assumptions unevenly at best. For example, a study of congregants at thirty-one Roman Catholic, Protestant Calvinist, and Protestant non-Calvinist churches found that the salience of their religious faith and church participation correlated significantly with their tendency to view work as a "calling."[8] However, specific denominational norms, sermons, and pastoral influence had little effect. Similarly, religious affiliation and religious conviction yield little or no correlation with organizational commitment, job satisfaction, job involvement, or achievement need.[9]

Yet cross-national research does suggest that the Protestant work ethic is alive and well, though not necessarily among Protestants. Comparative studies in Barbados, China, Malaysia, India, Sri Lanka, and Uganda have found a commitment to measures of the Protestant work ethic as strong or even stronger than those found in predominantly Protestant nations. This has led analysts to conclude that Weber's predisposition notwithstanding, many other religious and cultural traditions are rooted in analogous commitments to the centrality of work and to the accumulation of wealth through austerity and frugality.[10]

Matched by the industrial success of Far Eastern nations, notably Japan, this has led cross-cultural research to uncover themes in Eastern faiths that support and encourage work values similar to those of the Protestant work ethic. Elements of Confucianism, for example, are said to encourage respect for work, discipline, thrift, and duty in the maintenance of harmony and support for an ordered society. In addition, interpersonal principles such as *guanxi* (social connections and indebtedness) and *jen* (warm feeling between people) promote a high degree of organizational loyalty and close relationships among coworkers, and between employees and management.[11]

It is against this backdrop that we undertake an analysis of Jewish work values as they emerge in the classic texts. These will be derived from Hebrew Scripture, the Talmud and its commentaries, the medieval codes, and the collections of rabbinic responsa, the approximate equivalent of case law and legal findings developed by leading religious thinkers over the centuries. A concluding section will attempt to categorize these sources by the framework detailed above and provide specific suggestions for future research.

II

In the Bible, labor is introduced as a scourge and punishment to mankind. The narrative is well known (Genesis 2:15, 3:16–19). Adam and Eve are placed in the Garden of Eden to work and to protect it, restricted only in that they must refrain from eating of the Tree of Knowledge of Good and Evil and of the Tree of Life . Once they transgress the Lord's will by eating the forbidden fruit, they are expelled from the luxurious garden wherein their physical needs were divinely provided. Moreover, for Adam's personal iniquity, the land would be ever cursed before him. He would earn bread only "by the sweat of [his] brow." Despite his ministering, the earth would bring up only thorns and thistles.

Those seeking inspiration from this passage, or writing commentary to it, could easily have declared, therefore, that among Jewish values, work was a curse and a punishment. The need to toil was born in evil and rained upon hapless man only for the sins of his forebears. Indeed some traditional commentaries derived variations of this message, suggesting that with this scriptural narrative the role of human initiative was transformed. No longer could man assume that the Lord would provide of His bounty. No longer could man reach out and pluck what nature had prepared. Because of his sin, what he consumed would now depend largely upon his own efforts. He would eat, but only with great exertion.[12]

In more poetic form, consider the following talmudic lament:

> Rabbi Shimon ben Eliezer said, "Have you seen beast or fowl with a craft? Yet they are sustained without pain. Were they not created only to serve me? And I, who have been creat-

ed to serve my maker, should I not certainly subsist without pain? Except that I turned my deeds to evil, and my subsistence is curtailed."

(Kiddushin 82a)

In its natural state, life for man should be as effortless and carefree as it is for the beast or the bird of the field, who earn their bread with neither trade nor craft to support them. But because of his sin the effortless bounty man rightly deserves is curtailed, and because of his evil, he is subject to arduous labor.

Some refused to take the verse at its word. They redirected its meaning, even wresting it entirely from its context. They noted that the Lord's punishment to Adam was not prototypical. Rather than man himself, it was the land that had been cursed, and therefore the impact was limited to those who worked the fields.[13] In a creative leap, others inferred medicinal advice from this prescription. They noted the value of perspiration as a boon to the appetite and the digestion. To eat bread by the sweat of one's brow suggests that food is best consumed only after vigorous exercise.[14] Most significantly, normative rabbinic sources largely ignore this passage in their consideration of the place of work in the social scheme. Neither a curse nor purely an instrumental necessity of subsistence, they look upon it as an ennobling facet of moral development.

To affirm this proposition, some nine hundred "work-related statements" from the Babylonian and Jerusalem Talmud, the Tosefta, and nineteen compendia of the Midrash were recently reviewed and categorized. A quantitative content analysis was then executed to discern the norms and values represented by these statements. The results suggest that of all "ideational references" to the value of labor, 84 percent were positive, reflecting a "high esteem of work and craft." Evidently this esteem was intrinsic to labor and not merely a concession to the need to work as a condition for sustenance.[15]

To more fully develop an understanding of these values, a brief sampling of such statements is in order. For example, labor was so central to the rabbinic scheme for living that the two, work and life, were often equated in literary and poetic form. We read in Moses' famous soliloquy at the close of a lifetime as leader and lawgiver: "I bring the heavens and the earth as witness that life and death have I placed before you, blessing and curse. And you shall choose life so that you and your children may survive" (Deuteronomy 30:19).

Of the variety of messages the rabbis might have derived from the ringing call "choose life," it is telling that Rabbi Yishmael understood it to mean choosing a trade or a vocation (Talmud Yerushalmi, Pe'ah 1.1, Kiddushin 1:7). To earn one's keep by gainful employment is a central tenet of normal existence set in the crossroads between life and death, between blessing and curse. It was to be understood as livelihood in its literal sense, a mode for living.

In a similar conceit, the rabbis infer numerous lessons from Jethro's advice to Moses in regard to the administration of the people's needs and the resolution of their conflicts (Exodus 18:20). Among them is a curious reference to "the home of their lives," presumably to practices that sit at the root of their very existence. Rashi, in his commentary to the Talmud, understands this to mean both the study of religious texts (Bava Kamma 100b) as well as "a trade by which they can sustain themselves" (Bava Metzia 30b). Once again labor and vocation are equated with life itself, this time alongside the study of Torah.

At the same time, the talmudic sages tell us that one should love work and avoid positions of authority (Avot 1:10, Avot de Rabbi Natan 11:1), for as the Torah was given in a covenant with Israel, so too was gainful labor part of the covenant. As evidence they cite the verse "Six days shall you toil, and you shall do all your work, and the seventh day is a Sabbath for the Lord" (Exodus 19:8–9).

The proof-text is curious. More commonly, it stands among those invoked as a base for the institution of the Sabbath day and for its various obligations and restrictions. Rarely is it considered a mandate for the other six. The rabbis here seem to be suggesting that the six days of labor hold intrinsic religious value in rough parallel to the spiritual benefits derived from the Sabbath itself. Indeed, the Mishnah goes on to tell that Adam partook of the fruits of paradise only after he toiled in its fields, the commentary cited above notwithstanding. By the same token, in a later narrative the Lord would not allow His presence to rest among them before the Israelites labored in constructing His desert tabernacle.

Rabbi Yehudah and Rabbi Shimon both declare, "Great is work, for it brings honor to its master" (Nedarim 49b), while Rabbi Yirmiah proclaims that its value is more dear than noble ancestry (Bereshit Rabba 74:12). In that vein, consider the following from Rabbi Hiyya ben Ami in the name of Ulla:

> Greater is one who benefits from the work of his hands than he who stands in fear of heaven. Regarding the fear of heaven it is written: "Happy is the one who fears the Lord" (Psalms 112:1). However, in regard to the work of one's hands it is written: "If you eat by the work of your hands, happy are you and it will go well for you" (Psalms 128:2). Happy are you in this world, and it will go well for you in the world-to-come.
>
> (Berakhot 8a; see also Avot 4:1)

Here too the reference is curious. Rewards attributed to the "fear of heaven" should reasonably accrue in the spiritual or mystical realm of the world-to-come, whereas those attached to self-sufficiency should garner extra benefits in the more material clime of our mundane present. Yet the rabbis chose to understand these texts in reverse. The extra promise "that it shall go well" for one who toils on his own behalf is one of well-being in the celestial regions of eternal paradise.

The dissonance concerned Rabbi Shmuel Edels, whose commentary here serves to expands our point.[16] He relates the story of Rabbi Hanina ben Dosa (Ta'anit 25a), a saintly soul whose godliness was matched only by his indigence. At his wife's behest, the rabbi prayed that he and his family be adequately sustained through the mercy of heaven. His prayers were answered when he mysteriously discovered a golden pillar whose sale would support them for many years.

Soon thereafter Rabbi Hanina had a dream in which he was sitting among the saintly and pious of all ages around golden tables, imbibing the spirit of the Divine. To his shock, however, his table was absent a prop, the very golden pillar that had been bequeathed to support his family. Though his petition was just, his stake in Paradise was diminished. Again at his wife's behest, he prayed that golden pillar be returned to heaven. They would live in hunger and want rather than compromise their eternal rewards in the hereafter.

From this Rabbi Edels infers the moral lesson embedded in our dictum. One places his eternal reward at risk when piety forces dependence upon the largess of heaven. By contrast, he who provides for himself ensures that his faith and good deeds remain intact and stand him in good stead. To be self-sufficient, therefore, provides a spiritual benefit even over the fear of heaven. Beyond a mere prescription for comfortable living, it stands akin to a religious obligation.

III

The Talmud holds parents responsible to properly train and prepare their children for successful lives. Among the essentials in this relationship are the obligations to see that a child marries and to teach him a trade. To be negligent is tantamount to training one's child to be a thief (Kiddushin 29a–30b). A strong sentiment suggests that a life of commerce might not fulfill this obligation, for fear that one might resort to a life of crime if his business does not go well. The Tosefta (Kiddushin 1:8) and its commentaries extend this preference by indicating that the work of a merchant naturally leads him to walk the fringes of integrity and to seize opportunities that straddle the very margins of the law. In contrast, a trade or vocation protects its bearer. He will never be looked askance, nor will his neighbors question the legitimacy of his means of support.[17] Might this presage contemporary Jewry and its disproportionate penchant for the professions?

It should be noted that parental obligations were generally reserved for fathers and sons. As with many traditions, Jewish thought and the sages who were its arbiters presumed that the workplace would be a largely masculine environment. They maintained a fairly strict division of sex roles, with men acting as breadwinners and women holding court in the domestic sphere. It is no surprise, therefore, that in apportioning child-rearing responsibilities, vocational training was placed squarely within the paternal realm. By the same token, there is little in normative Jewish thought to preclude married women from working outside the home. Indeed there is much evidence that this was quite common among Jews in Europe and the New World in particular. Wives still retained supervisory responsibilities in the home, however, usually executed through the agency of various domestic servants in their employ.[18]

The obligation to seek vocational training for one's children is curious in other respects. The Talmud strains to find a legal source or proof-text for its grounding. It settles for a biblical verse adjuring one to "seek a life with the woman you love" (Ecclesiastes 9:9). Following the path hewn just above, the sages associate productive labor with successful living. Even as a rewarding life requires that one find a mate, they reason, so it demands that one be armed with a trade, and both fall within the obligations of parent to child. Proof-text aside, apparently this obligation was a deeply held value with a long tradition, whose authority superseded any grounding in text.

The absence of a clear scriptural base disturbed later authorities, however. They include other enumerated parental responsibilities in their normative codes, especially those of a more ritual nature. The obligation to teach a trade, however, is omitted. For example, Maimonides, Rabbi Yaakov Ba'al ha-Turim, and Rabbi Yosef Caro all agree that a father must take care that his son is circumcised and that he study Torah. If appropriate, he also must see that his son has undergone the *pidyon ha-ben* ceremony whereby a first-born male is "redeemed" for his family.[19]

Yet, despite an equally clear talmudic mandate, none of them rules directly that a father is obliged to teach his son a trade. A brief caveat is in order. The absence of such a ruling notwithstanding, these authorities do find it acceptable to discuss the vocational training of a child on the Sabbath, based on talmudic references elsewhere (Shabbat 150a, Ketubbot 5a). Evidently, they believe it to be in tune with a day whose spirit generally excludes the secular and mundane, a day reserved for religious fulfillment.[20] It is reasonable to assume, therefore, that they saw such training as a mitzvah, a divine obligation.

Indeed, one of the primary commentaries to Rabbi Caro's code makes that point precisely.[21]

Nevertheless, they do not include it among the normative duties of a parent. It seems that anyone may engage in such a task on the Sabbath, whether or not he has children. By the same token, a parent who neglects it on this day or any other is not to be judged delinquent. Notably many of their predecessors and teachers ruled to the contrary.[22]

A discordant note is sounded in the Talmud. At the very close of the tractate that houses much of this discussion, Rabbi Nehorai asserts: "I would leave all the trades in the world and teach my son nothing but Torah. The trades will not stand for him except in his youth. In his elder years he will be suspended in hunger. Not so Torah, which will stand for him in his youth and give him future and hope in his old age" (Kiddushin 82b).

A parallel statement by the same rabbi grounds his despair in the advent of physical incapacity: "When one comes to illness or old age or suffering, and no longer can tend to his work, then he shall die in hunger." Still, these sentiments, find no direct route into the rulings and codes of the major rabbinic authorities. They do, however, presage a lively debate over the proper balance between study and employment as a religious value and a life orientation. The issue will be considered at length in the next chapter.

IV

The rabbis of the Talmud also offered recommendations regarding the place of work in one's life and the nature or quality of the trade to be pursued. As a general rule they advised that one teach his son a clean and simple trade. Not the consuming passion of life, one's work should be seen as temporary and fleeting by comparison to the values of Torah and its commandments.

Parents were also warned against vocations that would bring their sons into close contact with women and might consequently facilitate immorality and threaten family life. Jewelers, tailors, perfumers, and sandlers are among those enumerated. Even teachers of primary-school children were cautioned because of their regular contact with the young mothers of their charges (Kiddushin 82a). Warnings also were issued about specific trades or professions, and the rabbis minced few words regarding the corruption of their practitioners.

For an example, the talmudic sage Abba Gurion questioned the integrity of those in the transport industry of his time, including merchant seamen, donkey and camel drivers, and the coopers who made barrels and containers for them. In his commentary, Rashi refers to their tendency to graze their beasts on the fields of unsuspecting landholders in their path and decries their willingness to compromise the conditions of their charge once they have journeyed far enough to escape their clients' scrutiny. Rabbi Shmuel Edels in his talmudic commentary claims that Abba Gurion intended no aspersion on their good faith per se. These trades should be avoided because they require long and arduous journeys that drive men far from their homes and families. He reserves his ire, however, for shopkeepers and retail merchants who deceive their customers, quite literally adding "water to the wine and stones to the wheat."

Rabbi Yehudah takes issue with Abba Gurion, sharpening some of his assessments while softening others. Most donkey drivers are evil and untrustworthy, he concedes, but not so the camel drivers. The latter must travel through the most desolate and threatening parts of the earth, and as Rashi explains, "break their hearts" in prayer so that the Lord will see them home in safety. Merchant sailors are the most pious of all because they are in constant danger and fully dependent upon the whim of the elements. They live by their faith and lean upon God's good will.[23]

Physicians are singled out for more bitter appraisals, an ironic twist given the popularity of the medical profession among Jews in our time. "The best of doctors be damned!" cries Rabbi Yehudah. The commentaries link this bitter assessment to the greed, insolence, and indifference physicians often arrogated unto themselves. As Rashi explains, they fear no illness and "never break their heart to the Lord." A physician "has in his power to heal the poor, but he heals not."

In an attempt to retrieve some of their dignity, Rabbi Shmuel Edels interprets the talmudic declaration not as a general assessment but as a stark warning to those who would enter the field. In his words:

It is proper that we interpret "the best of doctors [be damned]" to mean those who think themselves the best, experts with no peer. They depend upon their skill out of their own presumption. Sometimes they err on the nature of an illness and kill a patient with their remedies. Rather they must consult with other physicians and remember that lives are at stake.[24]

Finally, the purest of butchers are said to be "partners to Amalek," a reference to an ancient tribe that, by the scriptural account, carried out a surprise attack on the Israelites as they wandered through the desert after the exodus from Egypt. So heinous was this crime that the Lord decreed that the very memory of Amalek was to be blotted from the pages of history, and Jewish tradition requires that their treachery be recalled in a public reading each year. In what way are butchers their partners?

The commentaries are divided. Some insist that like those described in the preceding paragraphs, butchers succumb to greed and dishonesty. Poorly prepared foods or meats rendered ritually unfit often cross their path. To increase their profits, they overlook such infractions, misrepresenting their products and allowing their customers to transgress Jewish dietary laws in ignorance. They are guilty of theft even as they promote sin. Others maintain that butchers develop a cold, unfeeling attitude toward the creatures of the Lord and become indifferent to cruelty. Soon this cruelty penetrates their own nature and they become like Amalek.[25]

By and large, these teachings and their ramifications did not find their way into the normative codes of later authorities and appear to have little influence on occupational choices today. Nevertheless, they provide us with important ethical ideals regarding the choice of a career and the integrity that must stand at its core. Professional codes of ethics emerge from assessments such as these and from the experience upon which they are based.

V

Finally, apart from the choice of a career or one's exertion in its pursuit, the role of fate and fortune were considered important ingredients of prosperity. As noted, parents were not to direct their children toward trades that were consuming. Vocation should never overtake good deeds and faith as life's priority.

According to Rabbi Meir, "One should always teach his child a trade that is clean and simple, and then pray to the One in Whose hands reside both property and wealth. For there is no trade that is absent poverty or affluence. Neither does poverty or affluence depend upon one's trade, but rather everything is according to one's merit" (Kiddushin 82a).

The point much exercised the talmudic commentaries. In the first case, it appeared to contradict clear references to the contrary elsewhere in the Talmud. Thus the sage Rava tells us that "one's life span, children, and prosperity do not depend upon personal merit but rather upon *mazal*" (Mo'ed Katan 28a). Not easily defined, *mazal* popularly connotes luck or fate, though more precisely it refers to the astrological signs ascendant on the day and at the hour of birth. More recent talmudic commentaries have attempted to include a mix of social and biological factors, such as genetic makeup, upbringing, national culture, and nutrition, as correlates of this elusive variable.[26]

In Rava's view, therefore, the most fundamental elements of life—longevity, fecundity, and prosperity—were controlled less by man or even by heaven than by the stars, matters of simple and inalterable fate. His dictum is supported by several anecdotes regarding individual pietists and scholars of apparently similar merits whose success and good fortune varied sharply.

The issue parallels a lively discussion with numerous references in talmudic and later rabbinic literature. For example, Rabbi Hanina tells us that "it is *mazal* that brings wisdom and riches," and that all people, including adherents to the Jewish faith, are subject to its reign (Shabbat 156a). His assessment sums up an earlier discourse outlining at great length the influence of the celestial bodies in determining the character of those born on a given day of the week, or at a particular hour of the day (Shabbat 102b). Elsewhere, however, the same Rabbi Hanina explains that "all is in the hands of heaven except for the fear of heaven" (Berakhot 34a). This is generally understood to place fate in the hands of the Lord, leaving faith and morality to human choice and discretion.

Others demur, preferring to follow the path set by Rabbi Meir above. For them *mazal* may play a central role for much of humanity. However, owing to their special relationship with the Creator, adherents to Judaism are not governed by the movement of stars. For them success is a function of personal merit. Moral and spiritual accomplishment defines them and determines their financial success and prosperity. In a phrase infused with much irony among those who reflect on the adversities of Jewish history, Rabbi Yohanan declares, "There is no *mazal* for Israel" (see Shabbat 156a and Yevamot 70a).

Still, many talmudic commentaries remained unwilling to part with the idea that a profound influence on the vital aspects of life is exerted by *mazal*, this characteristic form of Jewish fate. Yet to claim that there was no recourse from what had been ordained at birth flew in the face of deeply held values of free choice and personal accountability. To ease the conflict, they argued that even for Jews, the broad social patterns of life, along with highly personal and individual dispositions, were predetermined. However, extraordinary effort in the form of prayer and supplication, joined with personal morality, religious study, and acts of kindness and compassion, may yet avert misfortune ordained. [27]

Their position was reinforced by such passages as the following: "What shall a man do so that he may become wealthy? Let him increase his business activities and trade. Let him buy and sell honestly and faithfully. Many have done such and it has not helped. Rather, let him beg for mercy from the One with Whom all wealth resides" (Niddah 70b).

What emerges, therefore, is a threefold formula whereby assiduous labor and honest trade combine with personal merit and with *mazal* to determine material success. Pursuing one to the exclusion of the others is a prescription for disappointment and failure. Hard work alone is no guarantor of wealth. In fact, it may actually hinder success if overemphasis makes it an obstacle to moral and spiritual improvement.

Similarly, merit and supplication may avert the penury or misfortune ordained by the stars—but then again, they may not. Therefore, one is warned to "increase his business activities," that is, to work hard and honestly. Yet he is not to lose faith, even if he sees see hard-working saints spending their lives in poverty while the evil prosper. *Mazal* remains part of the mix, and according to some, the determining factor. A fourth element, the Lord's compassion, remains available to those for whom the others have been insufficient.

The advice for parents to teach their children a trade that is simple and clean takes on fuller meaning in this context. Taken alone, neither one's choice of profession nor one's efforts in practicing it lead to wealth. Each field has its potential for success and for failure. There are elements of prosperity that simply cannot be controlled and misfortunes that will not be averted no matter how fervent the prayer or how sincere the penance. Therefore encourage children to choose a trade that is simple and clean, neither degrading nor exhausting, a trade that leaves ample time for religious reflection and study, a trade that will become neither life's central focus nor its driving force. Early on, teach them that poverty is a function of neither sloth nor indifference. A successful life is marked not by wealth and material acquisition but by spiritual values and personal morality.

VI

Clearly, there are numerous analogies between classical Jewish attitudes toward work and those ascribed by Weber to Protestant faith and Calvinist doctrine. While many of the commentaries to Hebrew Scripture understand the first chapters of Genesis as evidence that work is a curse and punishment to unfaithful man, this is largely ignored in normative Jewish thought. On the contrary, labor is looked upon as ennobling.

So central is it to successful living, that work and life are poetically equated, even in the minds of the same biblical commentaries. Indeed, in some formulations, labor emerges as a religious obligation with its own brand of spiritual fulfillment akin to that associated with the rest ordained on the Sabbath day. Moreover, financial self-sufficiency is to be valued above the fear of heaven, and those whose piety precludes such independence may actually threaten their eternal rewards in the world-to-come.

At the same time, early references place an obligation upon parents to prepare their children for the world of work, lest they abandon them to brigandage. Even business and commerce are looked askance, in favor of trades and professions that protect their practitioners both from the temptations of theft and the gossip of neighbors. Among these, the rabbis expressed specific preferences, reserving harsh comment for physicians, transport workers, and butchers. For the most part their derision stemmed from two bases of concern, one a function of the task itself and the other the attitudes and values it spawns.

They worried that certain trades naturally encouraged unethical or immoral behavior. Thus shopkeepers and traders are tempted to compromise their personal integrity or the quality of their goods in favor of increased profits. Employment in areas with largely female clientele would give way to sexual impropriety, they feared. They also expressed concern that physicians, for example, might fall prey to the arrogance they believed implicit to their profession, or butchers to the bloody cruelty their occupation engendered. They favored vocations close to the elements so that their practitioners could not but recognize their dependence upon forces far beyond their control. This, they believed, led to piety and simple religious faith, and lent a populist flavor to Jewish religious thought. The laborer is favored for his simple piety over the professional and the merchant who may be given to arrogance and presumption.

Yet here Jewish thought moves closer to ideals generally ascribed to classical Greece and early Christianity and at sharp contrast with Calvinism. Nowhere do we find obligations to reinvest profits and seek increased wealth as a form of religious fulfillment. Indeed, the very nature of the commercial endeavor is looked upon with some disdain. Moreover, the harsh determinism implicit in Calvin's idea of the elect is anomaly to a Jewish faith deeply rooted in existential free will and personal accountability. Jewish tradition exhibits a profound commitment to charity and compassion, seeing wealth as a gift over which one is little more than a conservator. There is nothing here to suggest that support for the needy is futile or somehow contrary to the divine will.

The direct link between hard work and financial success is also tenuous. In addition to an industrious demeanor, Jewish tradition sees personal merit and the illusive influence of *mazal* as equal or primary ingredients. If one seeks material reward, then surely he should increase his business activity and work hard. However, success will also depend on the honesty and integrity that one brings to business and professional activities. Yet many have done all this and have still not succeeded. For them a program of prayer, supplication, and good deeds may avail. Alas, even the most hardworking, honest, and saintly may suffer poverty and want owing to their lack of good fortune, which is in some measure governed by the stars and constellations.

Consequently, parents are urged to teach their children trades that are simple and clean, for it is not the trade alone that brings wealth but also the merit and the *mazal* of its practitioner. One is well advised, therefore, to invest time in winning favor with the Lord through acts of compassion, through prayer and religious contemplation, and through Torah study. According to some, this may even overtake fate written in the stars.

It may be helpful to borrow Hofstede's' four-part taxonomy detailed above as a summary framework here. Compared to the Protestant work ethic, Jewish thought appears less "masculine," placing lower value upon personal assertiveness as a factor in the accumulation of wealth. It also accords lesser priority to "individualism," defined as striving for personal success over the interest of the group. A life of simplicity and security is prescribed over one of risk and uncertainly, marking Jewish values lower on Hofstede's order of "uncertainty" as well. Finally, "power distance," unequal distributions of social status and influence, appear less tolerable than in Calvinist theology.

This is reflected in a small but growing body of empirical research regarding work values in Israel. Of course the cultural norms of Israeli society are not purely a function of Jewish faith. From the first, Zionist ideology emphasized the importance of hard work as a contribution to state-building efforts and to the modern renaissance of Jewish life. Moreover, in the socialist political expressions that dominated its early development, Zionism viewed manual labor as the route to emancipation and self-sufficiency. Consequently, to find that Israelis venerate work may reflect modern political thought more than peculiarly Jewish values.[28]

Yet a comparative study of work values in Israel, Germany, and Holland, the latter two nations with large Protestant populations, yielded interesting results.[29] Among German and Dutch workers, clear positive relationships emerged between work centrality and strong religious commitments or years of religious study. Consistent with Weber's hypothesis, this suggested the positive influence of Protestant ideals on work values. Among Israelis, religious conviction and religious education were negatively correlated with work centrality, suggesting that Jewish religious influences lead in an opposite direction.

Similarly, the sense of obligation to work, its intrinsic value, and the responsibility to save were all important among religious respondents from Germany and Holland but not among their Israeli counterparts. Rather, non-religious Israelis were most similar to religious respondents from the other two nations. To the extent that Jewish religious culture can be isolated in a cross-national study, it appears to influence adherents in a direction opposite to the norms of the Protestant work ethic.

Yet another important consideration remains. Alongside a generally positive attitude toward the importance of work and its role in normal living, Jewish texts speak with awe and reverence of those for whom "the Torah is their profession." Regular religious study and reflection is expected of all Jews.

However, a special place is reserved for those to whom it is an exclusive pursuit. Devoting oneself exclusively to the study and review of Torah laws, precepts, and traditions is held aloft as the model both for personal fulfillment and the survival of the faith. However, the relationship between such values and all that has been said thus far is by no means simple. Its vagaries and complexities will be explored in the next chapter.

1. Max Weber, *The Protestant Ethic and the Spirit of Capitalism* (New York: Scribner's, 1958).

2. This section is culled from the following sources: P. D. Anthony, *The Ideology of Work* (London: Tavistock, 1977); L. Braude, *Work and Workers* (New York: Praeger, 1975); M. Rose, *Reworking the Work Ethic: Economic Values and Socio-Cultural Politics* (London: Schocken, 1985); Gideon J. Rossouw, "Where Have All the Christians Gone?" *Journal of Business Ethics* 13, no. 7 (1994): 557–571; Richard Tawney, *Religion and the Rise of Capitalism* (New Brunswick, NJ: Transaction Books, 1998); A. Tilgher, *Homo Faber: Work Through the Ages* (New York: Harcourt Brace, 1930).

3. James Davidson and David P. Cadell, "Religion and the Meaning of Work," *Journal for the Scientific Study of Religion* 33, no. 2 (1994): 135–142; Seymour Martin Lipset, "The Work Ethic, Then and Now," *Public Interest* vol. 35 no. 4 (1990): 61–69; R. Preston, *The Future of Christian Ethics* (London: SCM, 1987).

4. See, e.g., Paul Bernstein, *American Work Values: Their Origin and Development* (Albany: State University of New York Press, 1997).

5. E.g., David McClelland, *The Achieving Society* (Princeton, N.J.: Van Nostrand, 1961); Gerhard Lenski, *The Religious Factor* (Garden City, N.Y.: Doubleday, 1963; Andrew Greeley, "The Protestant Ethic: Time for a Moratorium," *Sociological Analysis* 25 (1974): 20–33.

6. G. Hofstede, "Motivation, Leadership and Organization: Do American Theories Apply Abroad?" *Organizational Dynamics* 9 (1980): 42–63; idem, "The Cultural Relativity of Organizational Practices and Theories," *Journal of International Business Studies* 14, no. 2 (1983): 75–90; idem, *Culture and Organizations; Software of the Mind* (London: McGraw-Hill, 1991); idem, "Cultural Constraints on

Management Theories," *Academy of Management Executive* 7 (1993): 81–94.

7. For a review of these efforts, see Jennifer Dose, "Work Values: An Integrative Framework and Illustrative Application to Organizational Socialization," *Journal of Occupational and Organizational Psychology* 70, no. 3 (1997)): 219–240; MOW International Research Team, *The Meaning of Work* (London: Academic Press, 1987); A. Furnham, *The Protestant Work Ethic: The Psychology of Work Related Beliefs and Ethics* (London: Routledge, 1990); A. Furnham and M. Rose, "Alternative Ethics: The Relationship Between the Wealth, Welfare, Work and Leisure Ethic," *Human Relations* 40 (1987): 561–574.

8. James Davidson and David Caddell, "Religion and the Meaning of Work," *Journal for the Scientific Study of Religion* 33, no. 2 (1994): 135–142. See also James Lincoln and Arne Kalleberg, "Work and Work Force Commitment: A Study of Plants and Employment in the US and Japan," *Sociological Review* 30 (1985): 738–760.

9. Leonard Cushmir and Christine Koberg, "Religion and Attitudes Toward Work: A New Look at an Old Question," *Journal of Organizational Behavior* 9 (1988): 251–262.

10. For a review of this research, see F. S. Niles, "Toward a Cross Cultural Understanding of Work Related Beliefs," *Human Relations* 52, no. 7 (1999): 855–867; A. Furnham et al., "A Comparison of Protestant Work Ethic Beliefs in Thirteen Nations," *Journal of Social Psychology* 133, no. 2 (1993): 185–197.

11. David A. Ralston, "Doing Business in the 21st Century with the New Generation of Chinese Managers: A Study of Generational Shifts in Work Values in China," *Journal of International Business Studies* 30, no. 2 (1999): 415–428; Jing-Lih Farh, Anne Tsui, Katherine Xin, and Bor-Shiuan Cheng, "The Influence of Relational Demography and Quanxi: The Chinese Case," *Organizational Science* 9, no. 4 (1998): 471–488; Lisa Hope Peled and Katherine Xin, "Work Values and Their Human Resource Management Implications: A Theoretical Comparison of China, Mexico and the United States," *Journal of Applied Management Studies* 6, no. 2 (1997): 185–198; David A. Ralston, "The Impact of National Culture and Economic Ideology on Managerial Work Values: A Study of the United States, Russia,

Japan and China," *Journal of International Business Studies* 28, no. 1 (1997): 177–208; Norman Coates, "The 'Confucian Ethic' and the Spirit of Japanese Capitalism," *Leadership and Organizational Development Journal* 2, no. 3 (1987): 17–23.

12. See, e.g., the notations of Rashi, Ibn Ezra, and Seforno to Genesis 3:19.

13. R. Yehudah he-Hasid, cited in *Da'at Zekenim mi-Ba'alei ha-Tosafot*, Genesis 3:19.

14. *Klei Yakar* Genesis 3:19.

15. Bilha Mannheim and Avraham Sela, "Work Values in the Oral Torah," *Journal of Psychology and Judaism* 15, no. 4 (1991): 241–259.

16. Rabbi Shmuel Edels, *Aggadot Maharsha*, Berakhot 8a

17. Also see *Minhat Bekurim* commentary to Tosefta Kiddushin 1:8.

18. Hanita Blumfield, "Jewish Women Sew the Union Label," *Humanity and Society* 6, no. 1 (1982): 33–45; Ruth J. Markowitz, *My Daughter, the Teacher: Jewish Teachers in the New York City School System* (New York, 1981); Irene D. Neu, "The Jewish Business Woman in America" *American Jewish Historical Quarterly* 66, no. 1 (1976): 137–154; Jenna W. Joslit, "Saving Souls: The Vocational Training of American Jewish Women, 1880–1930" in *An Inventory of Promises: Essays in Honor of Moses Rischin*, ed. Jeffrey S. Gurock and Marc Lee Raphael, 151–169. Brooklyn: Carlson, (1995).

19. Rabbi Moshe Maimonides, *Yad ha-Hazakah*, Hilkhot Milah 3:1, Hilkhot Bikurim 11:1, Hilkhot Talmud Torah 1:1; Rabbi Yaakov Ba'al ha-Turim, *Tur*, Yoreh De'ah 260, 305:1, 205:1; Rabbi Yosef Caro, *Shulhan Arukh*, Yoreh De'ah 260, 305:1, 205:1.

20. Rabbi Moshe Maimonides, *Yad ha-Hazakah*: Hilchot Shabbat 24:5; Rabbi Yosef Caro, *Shulhan Arukh*, Orah Hayyim 306:6.

21. Rabbi Avraham Gombiner, *Magen Avraham*: Orah Hayyim 306:13.

22. E.g., Rashi, Shabbat 150a and Ketubbot 5a, s.v. *le-lamdo umanut*; Rabbi Yitzhak Alfasi, Kiddushin 12a; Rabbi Asher ben Yehiel, *Kitzur Piskei ha-Rosh*, Kiddushin 2:43.

23. Rashi, Kiddushin 82a, s.v. *hamar, gamal*; Rabbi Shmuel Edels, *Aggadot Maharsha*, Kiddushin 82a, s.v. *lo yilmad*.

24. Rabbi Shmuel Edels, *Aggadot Maharsha*, Kiddushin 82a, s.v. *tov she-ba-rofim*.

25. See, e.g., Rashi, Kiddushin 82a, s.v. *tov she-batabahim*; and *Tosafot Ri ha-Zaken*, Kiddushin 82a, s.v. *she-batabahim*.

26. See Tosafot Mo'ed Katan 28a, s.v. *elah be-mazalah*; and *Tiferet Yisrael*, Kiddushin 4:14, s.v. *lefi zekhut*.

27. See, e.g., Tosafot, Shabbat 156a, s.v. *ain mazal le-yisrael*; Rashi, Yevamot 70a, s.v. *zakhah mosifin lo*; Tosafot, Yevamot 70a, s.v. *mosifin lo*; also see Tosafot Kiddushin 82a, s.v. *elah ha-kol*; Tosafot, Mo'ed Katan 28a, s.v. *elah be-mazalah*; Aggadot ha-Maharsha: Mo'ed Katan 28a, s.v. *be-mazalah talia*.

28. See, e.g., Arthur Hertzberg, *The Zionist Idea: A Historical Analysis and Reader* (New York: Atheneum, 1975).

29. Itzhak Harpaz, "The Transformation of Work Values in Israel," *Monthly Labor Review* 122, no. 5 (1999): 46–51; idem, "A Cross National Comparison of Religious Conviction and the Meaning of Work," *Cross Cultural Research* 32, no. 2 (1988):143–170.

4

Torah Is Their Trade

I

In his musical soliloquy, Tevye the milkman, the hero of *Fiddler on the Roof,* opines the fact that the Lord has chosen to make him a poor laborer, withholding the joys and comforts of affluence. "If I were a rich man," he fantasizes, he would own a fine home with servants and livestock, and would be respected, honored, even fawned over, by the "most important men in town." Then a wistful look settles on his face and he sighs:

> If I were rich I'd have the time that I lack,
> To sit in the synagogue and pray
> And even have a seat by the eastern wall.
> And I'd discuss the holy books with the learned men
> Seven hours every day,
> Ah, that would be the sweetest thing of all!

At the roots of Jewish tradition are similar dreams about a life devoted to the full-time study of sacred texts and their commentaries, exclusive of the mundane and material responsibilities of the workaday world. One well-known talmudic passage, used to open the daily prayers, suggests that the study of Torah is equal to all other commandments combined

(Pe'ah 1:1, Shabbat 127a). Over time, special provisions were made to accommodate those for whom "Torah is their trade," including public support for their families so that they might pursue their studies unburdened by worldly concerns. Indeed the talmudic definition of a large city is one in which there were at least ten *batlanim,* or "free-riders, " who would spend their days in study and reflection, also performing various communal functions and ensuring that there was always a *minyan,* a religious quorum for prayer (Megillah 5a).[1]

Today the question of the gainful employment of such *batlanim* has become an explosive manifestation of the rift between Israel's secular majority and its growing communities of pietists, known as *haredim.* Those who must appear at work each day are appalled that increasing numbers of able-bodied young men devote their most productive years to religious study at yeshivot and kollelim, comprehensive programs of higher Jewish study. Exempted from most civic obligations, they are supported by the dole and by philanthropic largess. Sons are generally raised to follow in the footsteps of their fathers, while daughters are groomed for husbands who will do the same.

For their part, members of these haredi communities believe that they protect and ensure the Jewish future by devoting themselves to the study of Torah and by implanting the selfsame commitment in their children and grandchildren. Menial tasks and mundane details, among which most labor is included, are little more than *bittul Torah,* quite literally "Torah cancelled or wasted." The Lord demands that Jews spend their every waking hour in study and prayer, and they are living that ideal.[2]

The issue is linked to a series of parallel debates over draft deferments for able-bodied Israeli youth. Since the establishment of the state, military service has been a symbol of political and nationalist fidelity in defense of home and country. It also serves as a tool for the integration of a diverse population and as a proving ground for career success and upward mobility. Data gathered by the Israel Defense Force suggest that about thirty thousand young men, or some 7.4 percent of the conscript pool, are currently exempted from the military as yeshiva students. Projections suggest that the figure will rise to over 10 percent, or about thirty-five thousand, within two years. Under the current terms of their deferments, these students may not perform any work for pay, even if they leave their seminaries. As a result, they must depend upon public funds to support themselves and their growing families.

In December 1998 Israel's High Court of Justice rendered a decision giving Parliament one year to draft legislation correcting this imbalance. Presumably such a plan would reduce the number of deferments and pave the way for seminarians to enter some form of military service.[3] At this writing, amidst lively debate over the wisdom of the plan, experimental Nahal paramilitary units have been created to accommodate the special religious and social needs of these conscripts. The move has met resistance from both sides, with haredi advocates arguing that the military can never be an appropriate place for pietist youth, while secularists demand that all potential recruits be treated alike without accommodation.

Nevertheless, military authorities expect the effort to grow to battalion size. The first platoon was inducted during the winter of 1999, a second the following autumn, and a third early the next year, for a total of approximately two hundred recruits. Military sources indicate that these include haredi volunteers from Brooklyn and Los Angeles.[4]

In the United States the lines are not so sharply drawn, but strains are beginning to show. A growing number of middle-aged parents in the Orthodox Jewish community, who once expected that their filial obligations would be fulfilled upon the marriage of their children, are now called upon to continue supporting married offspring who have made full-time commitments to the religious study hall. At the same time public appeals are launched on behalf of programs of higher Jewish study, frequently offshoots of existing institutions. Difficult decisions of priority ensue for individual philanthropy, and for the allocation of limited and dwindling community resources.

In truth, the issue has been debated for tens of centuries with each side exhibiting notable passion, condemning and rebuking its adversaries in no uncertain terms. In this chapter we will examine some of the sources that inform this debate in hopes of clarifying the relationship between work and study in Jewish tradition. As we will show, there is ample precedent in talmudic and rabbinic sources both for those who favor a balance between the workplace and the study hall, and for those who demand a life of Torah learning exclusively.

However, we also will demonstrate that the latter was generally reserved for the singular and exceptional scholar. In contrast, most authorities appear to favor a balance between work and study as the modal prescription for successful living, appropriate for the vast majority of the faithful. Indeed, even the exceptional scholar was encouraged to seek financial self-sufficiency and to devote himself to his studies only after obtaining material support privately from individual sponsors and patrons.

In this vein it is worth noting a unique attempt to evaluate quantitatively the relative valence accorded to employment and learning in Jewish sources. Using expert reviewers,

Mannheim and Sela categorized some nine hundred "work-related statements" from the Babylonian and Jerusalem Talmuds, the Tosefta, and nineteen compendia of the Midrash. Included were statements favoring a combination of work and study, others that favored study alone, and even a handful that appeared to favor work over study.

After winnowing redundant and marginal examples, they labeled about half the final population of these dicta "laws," that is, binding obligations. The rest were identified as "norms" or "values." A systematic content analysis then was executed to determine the place of work in Jewish tradition as expressed in these texts. Among their findings, the following is most relevant to our purposes here.

> The internal distribution of the "Work and Torah" category reveals that in 65% of the quotations it is prescribed that the learning of Torah and work should be pursued jointly. In 29% of the statements, the learning of Torah is prescribed and in 6% work is preferred over Torah.[5]

What follows is a qualitative exploration of this relationship along with the implications for the direction and organization of the contemporary Jewish community and the allocation of its resources.

II

The Talmud records a lively debate that speaks directly to our issue (Berakhot 35b). It is based in the sages' reading of the biblical verse "and I shall give you rain in its season, early and later, and you shall gather your grain" (Deuteronomy 11:14), as against "and the words of the Torah shall not be absent from your mouth, and you shall be immersed in them day and night so that you guard all that is written therein. For then your path shall be successful and you shall grow wise" (Joshua 1:8).

The interlocutors are bothered by the apparent contradiction. Can one gather grain, both literally and figuratively toiling at his work, and yet still remain constantly immersed in the words of Torah? The answer, concludes Rabbi Yishmael, is to read these words in "the way of the world"; that is to say, these obligations ought not to be understood literally. Work must be combined with study. Otherwise, to paraphrase Rashi's commentary, one will become dependent upon the charity of others and neglect study entirely.

Rabbi Shimon ben Yohai thinks otherwise:

> Can it be that a person shall plow in season and plant in season and harvest in season and mill in season and plant in the wind? What shall become of Torah? Rather, when Israel fulfills the will of the Lord, their work will be performed by others. . . . When Israel does not fulfill the will of the Lord, then they must perform their own labor . . . and more, the work of others must they also perform.

Several points are in order. Rabbi Shimon's position evokes the plight of primordial man in the Garden of Eden. Here too worldly toil is cast as a form of punishment heaped upon man for his sin. If the people of Israel would only follow the ways of the Lord by devoting their time to the singular study of His holy books, they would be freed of such mundane obligations. Absent this commitment, menial labor emerges to fill the breach.

Rabbi Shimon's impatience with what Rabbi Yishmael terms "the way of the world" is clear from anecdotes related elsewhere. The best-known of them illustrates our point with powerful imagery (Shabbat 33b). We are told that Rabbi

Shimon was overheard making disparaging remarks about the Roman overlords of Judea. Forced to flee, he sought refuge first in his study hall and then in a cave. There, along with his son, Rabbi Elazar, he devoted himself exclusively to Torah study for twelve long years, sustained by God's compassion in the miraculous appearance of a spring and a carob tree.

He and his son emerged from the cave only after receiving word that their persecutors had relented. Forced to acclimate themselves to normal human society once more, the two rabbis were shocked at the sight of farmers and workmen going about their daily business, plowing, sowing, and harvesting. "They forsake eternal life and occupy themselves with passing needs," Rabbi Shimon said, horrified.

The two were so filled with anger that, by the talmudic account, everything caught in their gaze burst into flame. In short order, a voice boomed from the heavens, demanding that they return to the cave lest they destroy the world by their passion and their righteous indignation.

Rabbi Shimon was not yet ready to accept the demands placed upon those less exalted. He and his son went into seclusion once more, their confinement no longer a sanctuary from Roman oppression but more a form of divine penalty. They remained in the cave for an additional twelve months, the sentence imposed, by tradition, upon the most evil in purgatory. When they emerged once more, they again encountered peasants and villagers pursuing their livelihood. As before, flames burst forth from Rabbi Elazar's penetrating glance, but this time his father rushed to heal the wounds.

"The world has enough with you and me alone," Rabbi Shimon told his son, suggesting that not everyone need copy their model of staunch discipline and rigor. Subsequently they spied an old farmer, gathering myrtle from his harvest for the

Sabbath. His simple piety, combining the work ethic with devotion to the Lord's command, assuaged them and calmed their fiery spirit. Now the two rabbis could reenter society without undermining its foundations.

Evidently, Rabbi Shimon, a man of unbending principle and strict demeanor, was initially unable to accept a merger of fealty to God's will with "the way of the world." The fire in his soul threatened to consume the natural order, and he was banished to the cave by nothing less than divine decree. One with such a singular commitment, no matter how pure and sanctified, must live out his years divorced from society. The inference and the narrative that supports it fit neatly into the views expressed in Rabbi Shimon's debate with Rabbi Yishmael. If one plows and sows, then "what shall become of Torah?"

Yet his scriptural reading disquiets the commentaries. For them, it is ironic to claim, as he does, that the verse "and you shall gather your grain" is meant as a warning or a penalty. Both from its use elsewhere on the very same talmudic page, and from the verse that immediately precedes it, the phrase is clearly meant as the promise of reward to those who "shall surely listen to My commandments." How can Rabbi Shimon construe its meaning to the contrary?[6]

In an attempt to make peace with his assertions, the sages conclude that for Rabbi Shimon too, the phrase promises reward, albeit an imperfect one. Righteousness incomplete, condemns one to "gather his own grain," distracting him from the more elevated pursuits of study and prayer that should properly occupy his time. By contrast, those of impeccable faith and conduct shall have others to toil on their behalf.

A parallel debate between Rabbi Yishmael and Rabbi Shimon (Menahot 99b) has been marshaled to shed light on our discussion. On its face it appears to be the mirror image of our text, and in the minds of some it threatens to turn ours on its head. There Rabbi Shimon concurs that to study "day and night" one need merely read the words of the Shema, a biblical prayer recited twice daily, morning and evening. This contrasts sharply with his much more stringent demands above. Indeed, he concedes that the point ought not to be promoted, lest the ignorant employ it to free themselves of the obligation to study or to teach their children.

In a subsequent talmudic anecdote, Rabbi Yishmael is asked whether one may devote himself to "Greek wisdom." Citing the requirement to indulge in Torah day and night, he replies that other studies may be undertaken only during an hour that is neither day nor night. By implication there is room for nothing except Torah study, a position much in contrast with his far more liberal and expansive views cited above.

Recent commentaries vary in their attempts to blunt the apparent contradiction. The more direct argue that there is no contradiction at all. In this latter context, the two rabbis are dealing with very different circumstances. Rabbi Shimon, for example, is merely agreeing that one might fulfill his base obligation to study "day and night" by reciting a prayer whose regimen meets that timing. His demand to abandon job obligations in favor of study and to expect that proxies will perform his work is an ideal far beyond the scope of any other discussion. For his part, Rabbi Yishmael is responding to a request for license to explore "Greek wisdom," a highly suspect branch of knowledge. His response need not be understood in any broader vein. It certainly implies no ban on gainful employment in favor of study.[7]

Issuing no comment on the cogency of any of these sources, the Talmud draws conclusions grounded in common experience (Berakhot 35a). The sage Abbaye declares that many have followed the advice of Rabbi Yishmael and succeeded. By contrast, of those who followed Rabbi Shimon ben Yohai, many did not. As a practical matter, the Talmud seems to be suggesting that a balanced relationship between Torah study and gainful employment is a more likely recipe for personal success. At most Rabbi Shimon's strictures are reserved for the very few. One would be well advised not to pursue such a path, lest he be undone by his own presumptions. Indeed, elsewhere Rabbi Shimon testifies, "I have seen those who rise high, and they are but few," adding that they may possibly include only himself and his son (Sukkah 45b). The Talmud appears to accept his general principle, though it works hard to deflect the personal nature of his claim.

Finally, it is appropriate to conclude this facet of our discussion with two well-known citations from Avot, an early talmudic collection of ethical teachings and homilies that will figure handily in our later analysis. First,

> Rabban Gamliel son of Rabbi Yehudah the Prince said, "Better is the study of Torah with derekh eretz, for the effort expended in the two will keep sin out of mind. All Torah that is not accompanied by work ultimately will be nullified and cause sin." (Avot 2:2)

As above, *derekh eretz*, literally "the way of the world," is a euphemism for employment and the pursuit of livelihood. Here Rabban Gamliel advises that when pursued in tandem with study, each is strengthened. Unlike Rabbi Shimon, there is no consideration even for the few that may succeed at a life of study alone. Work serves as a necessary component to successful religious fulfillment. Study alone will be nullified. Ironically, it even may lead one astray.

The commentaries support the point by noting that one

searching for salvation solely by virtue of his learning will soon be left with no sustenance. He may come to abandon his studies and depend upon gambling, thievery, and deception for his bread.[8]

Beyond this, Rabbi Zadok tells us:

> Do not use them [words of Torah] as a crown by which to be glorified or a shovel with which to dig. And so Hillel would say, "One who uses the Torah as his trade shall be removed." From this we learn that any who derive benefit from the words of Torah remove their lives from the world.
>
> (Avot 4:5)

Quite apart from encouraging a life program that combines gainful employment and religious study, this source looks with disdain upon those who would support themselves through their learning. The words of Torah must remain pristine and pure, pursued for intrinsic value and not as a tool with which to justify one's keep. To do otherwise demeans their sanctity and "removes" one from the world. In a parallel sentiment, students are warned not to seek honor or tribute for their wisdom, never learning so that others might call them master and they can spend their days in the academy (Nedarim 62a). As we shall demonstrate, the sentiment grounded in these texts helped fuel the next stage of the debate.

III

The growing controversy over these alternative routes to successful living continued among later Jewish scholars. Throughout, however, those in the mainstream insisted that *derekh eretz*, the pursuit of livelihood in combination with religious study, was to be preferred for the bulk of the population. For example, following the path defined just above, Maimonides minced few words in expressing his utter disdain for those who accept public support in order to devote themselves exclusively to learning.

> Whomsoever has in his heart that he shall indulge in the study of Torah and do no work but rather be sustained from charity, defames the Lord's name, cheapens the Torah, extinguishes the light of faith, causes himself ill, and removes himself from the world-to-come. For it is forbidden that one benefit from words of Torah in this world. . . .
> . . . all Torah that is not accompanied by work will be nullified and end in sin. Ultimately such a person will steal from others. One is at a high level if he is sustained by the efforts of his own hand, a characteristic of the pious of early generations. In this he will merit all the honor and good of this world and the world-to-come, as it is written, "If you eat by the work of your hands, happy are you, and it will go well for you" (Psalms 128:2). Happy are you in this world, and it will go well for you in the world-to-come.[9]

In his commentary to the words of Rabbi Zadok, Maimonides enumerates the many scholars and sages who performed menial labor rather than accept philanthropic aid. Surely the wealthy of their generation would never have withheld their assistance but for the fact that able-bodied scholars refused to accept it. They saw no difficulty in suspending their study temporarily so that they could labor on behalf of their families and households, always remembering that work was transitory in life, whereas Torah was its foundation. Those who bring evidence to the contrary, Maimonides concludes, are "insane and confused."

His argument and the passion with which it was declared raised a storm of protest. Rabbi Yosef Caro, in his *Kesef Mishneh* commentary to Maimonides, strained to refute the Master's claim point by point. From earliest times scholars had sustained themselves through their learning, he countered, whether as students, teachers, or religious functionaries. To be sure, those who enter the field only to reap its benefits were to be condemned, alongside those with the means to support themselves but who accept charity nonetheless. However, those devoted to religious study purely "for the sake of heaven" deserved no such castigation. The community was obliged to support them.

He concludes his lengthy discourse by noting that practice and usage should serve as the arbiters of tradition, guiding our actions at every turn. Perhaps the sages of prior generations agreed in principle that students should not reduce themselves to dependence upon charity and the dole. Yet nowadays a preoccupation with the demands of a trade or profession would cause Torah learning to be forgotten and abandoned. Consequently, they amended their thinking and made provisions to encourage those who spend their lives exclusively in study. Else why would there be so many examples, both before and since, of precisely that practice which Maimonides seeks to defame?[10]

Rabbi Caro was joined by Rabbi Shimon ben Tzemach Duran, a fifteenth-century scholar in Spain and North Africa. He was scandalized by the aspersions being cast upon generations of scholars properly maintained by communal funds. In his words, Maimonides:

> broke his good senses and miscast all the scholars and rabbis of his time and those who preceded him. And because he

spoke in anger he came to err and to call them insane. Is a prophet insane, or is the man of God's spirit?

It was his [Maimonides'] good fortune to be close to royalty and honored in his generation, and because of his medical wisdom he was not required to accept fees from the communities he served. What shall rabbis and sages do if they have not reached this quality? Shall they die of hunger, demean their honor, and remove the yoke of Torah from their backs? That is not the intent of Torah, the commandments, or the Talmud.[11]

Notwithstanding the zealous indignation expressed by both sides, the less passionate rulings of their contemporaries generally reinforced the obligation of scholars to seek their own livelihood and avoid becoming wards of the community. Often they entered the debate tangentially, in response to unrelated demands and petitions, however. Representative examples of these findings deserve a brief digression, if only for the bits of social history they reveal.

One, dating to the thirteenth century, deals with a learned scholar who was libeled by a member of his community and took his allegations to the Gentile authorities. Upon investigation, the claims made by this scoundrel were proven false and the sage was exonerated of any wrongdoing. In the action that followed, the scholar sought damages for his defamation.

The case came before Rabbi Asher ben Yehiel (Rosh), of Germany and Spain, who found for the claimant and substantiated the damages committed by the defendant against him. However, the matter of setting specific financial liability turned upon the claimant's status as a scholar, that is, one fully devoted to Torah study. As if to forestall any further aspersions against him, Rabbi Asher provided the following definition of a scholar:

That his Torah is his craft, and that he sets regular periods for
Torah and cancels none of his studies, except for his maintenance. For it is impossible for him to learn without maintenance, for "if there is no flour there is no Torah," and "all Torah
that is not accompanied by work ultimately will be nullified and
cause sin." . . . The rest of the day, when he is free and is not
required to seek after his maintenance, he returns to his books
and studies, and he never strolls in the markets and roadways
but for his livelihood and that of his household. Nor should he
labor to accumulate much money. This I call a scholar.[12]

Though afield of the petition, Rabbi Asher provided us with
a clear statement of the responsibilities of one who dons the
exalted robes of Torah scholarship. Of course, he was expected
to commit himself to Torah study, but not to the exclusion of
his mandate to support himself and his family. If he wasted
none of his time, nor allowed such pursuits to overtake him,
his status was secure and he deserved the financial redress
appropriate to that station.

A second communal controversy several centuries later
sheds similar light upon the work values held dear even for
one pursuing the life of a scholar. Judging from the number of
rulings issued on the topic and the fervent zeal evident in their
language, the matter plainly engendered much vehemence on
both sides. Some background is in order.

The position of pre-modern Jewish communities was frag-
ile, precarious, and unenviable on several grounds. Isolated as
a separate social entity, they lived among, yet apart from, the
indigenous population. Jews were most often expected to
organize, regulate, and support their own communal services
with little assistance from municipal or regional authorities. In
addition, they were subject to special taxes and levies paid in
direct tribute to the local nobility or ecclesiastical leadership.

In effect, these served as protection payments to secure sanctuary, armed defense, and safe passage against the violent passions of the citizenry. As a result, Jews were particularly vulnerable to the fiscal whim of nobles seeking funds to enrich their treasuries or finance wars, explorations, and other risky ventures. At the least, both as a community and as individuals, they were forced to bear the burden of harsh, unreasonable, and discriminatory taxes.

Jewish leaders were much pressed, therefore, to raise revenues from every imaginable source, and that included the income of local rabbis and scholars. This flew in the face of long-standing Jewish tradition and practice. Apart from the universal obligations of charity and philanthropy, members of the clergy were exempted from municipal taxes and other forms of revenue generation, regardless of their own financial holdings or business pursuits. In this, the sides stood in mirrored parallel to the contemporary debate, virtually turning it on its head.

Lay and communal authorities evidently held, Rabbi Asher's dictum notwithstanding, that a scholar's life was to be devoted totally to his Torah studies, excluding all other activities, especially any that generated income. One who pursued gainful employment in the secular marketplace could no longer claim that "Torah was his trade." He was not a genuine scholar and had to pay his fair share. At the very least, funds generated by his commercial pursuits should be taxable, not exempted by clergy status.

For their part, rabbinic thinkers staunchly supported the clergy exemption, and it is here that the affair becomes relevant to our discussion. They consistently defended the pursuit of financial self-sufficiency by Torah students as a legitimate aim for their life's pursuit. In no way did it diminish their status as religious scholars or their claim to membership in the heady cadre of those for whom "Torah was their trade." To the contrary, they saw it as self-evident that Torah scholars had a moral obligation to support themselves rather than depend upon charitable assistance. If the large number of rulings on the issue is any indication, however, it appears that the rabbis were under great strain to impress this point upon their congregants.

The writings of Rabbi Mordechai Halevi of seventeenth-century Egypt eloquently represent these opinions. He goes so far as to term a scholar's pursuit of livelihood a mitzvah, a religious commandment. Thus:

> The studies that deal with the exemption of rabbis from tax and other forms of levy, how were they expressed? Did they refer to those who go begging from door to door? Did they speak of ministering angels that neither eat nor drink and have no bodily needs? It is written openly that one should do all manner of work, even what is strange to him, rather than depend upon others. . . .
>
> From all the studies we learn that the talmudic sages exempted rabbis absorbed in Torah, not meaning that they did not toil for their food and sustenance and the sustenance of their household. Rather, they exempted those who fulfilled the verse "and you shall be immersed in [Torah] day and night," according to their power and their abilities. They exempted those who did not suspend the words of Torah except to fulfill a mitzvah, to seek after their food and their sustenance and the sustenance of their household and their food.[13]

His sentiments echo those earlier expressed by colleagues and predecessors from Austria, France, Turkey, Greece, and Palestine over a period of three hundred years.[14]

IV

The debate and the controversy notwithstanding, mainstream Jewish attitudes, as reflected in normative codes of practice, appear fairly consistent. Thus Rabbi Yaakov ben Asher Ba'al ha-Turim, in his codification of laws and traditions, cites Maimonides almost verbatim, insisting upon financial self-sufficiency for scholars and students alike. Rabbi Yosef Caro, in his *Bet Yosef* commentary to Rabbi Yaakov's code, softens this ruling, consistent with his notes on Maimonides cited above. Again he argues that scholars are within their rights to accept public support even as communities are well advised to provide it. He concedes, however, that those able to see to their own material needs should refrain from accepting public funds, as a sign of piety and godliness.[15]

Yet in his own collection of laws and traditions, Rabbi Caro takes another path. Following Rabbi Yaakov's code, Rabbi Caro employs two categories to deal with the topic at hand. In one he considers customs and practices regarding the study of Torah, educational methodology, and the relationship between students and their instructors. Despite his vigorous defense of publicly supported scholarship, he simply ignores the matter of study and employment entirely. The breach much exercised those who, in turn, wrote companion notes to his code.

Concerned that Rabbi Caro's silence on this point might be misinterpreted as a concession to Maimonides and his supporters, they strained to reinforce the importance of undistracted Torah study, citing earlier authorities to fill the gap. Consider the following from two such commentaries:

One who studies at the academy, expands Torah publicly, and sets aside time for himself and for the needs of others, cannot leave his house except for matters of mitzvah. It is sinful for him not to accept support from others even if he is wise and able to profit and support his household on his own.[16]

Through this the Torah will be sustained among its students [if] they shall not be required to cancel their studies because of the demands of livelihood. Even those who have money of their own are still permitted [to collect from the public], for we cannot say that they have enough to survive. . . . The needs of Jews are great, to raise children as scholars and to marry daughters to scholars.[17]

By contrast, Rabbi Moshe Isserles, whose legal decisions formed the basis for most East European Jewish practice, gives full vent to the other side of the argument. He warns that Torah should always be the anchor of one's pursuits, since business dealings are never more than transitory. Yet, in words familiar by now, he adds that to be self-sufficient is a sign of piety and godliness. Though he concedes that some believe otherwise, one is prohibited from profiting from words of Torah unless old or infirm. Great is he who sustains himself, he declares, and, quoting Maimonides by way of Rabbi Yaakov Ba'al ha-Turim, one who studies in the expectation of doing no labor but being supported by charity defames the Lord and demeans the Torah.[18]

His reserve here notwithstanding, Rabbi Caro takes a more definitive stand on the issue in its other incarnation relative to the daily regimen of Jewish religious observance. His thrust seems to contradict his writings elsewhere, as he rules that after fulfilling the ritual obligations of prayer and supplication each morning, the believer is obliged to leave for the job.

"Torah that is not accompanied by work," he writes, quoting from the passage in Avot cited above, "will ultimately be nullified." He closes with a stern warning that all one's dealings must ever be honest and faithful.[19]

The decision is a rather straightforward statement in support of gainful employment from one of the primary advocates of undistracted Torah study. Still, modern authorities have interpreted it in ways that allow the millennial debate to continue. On the one hand, Rabbi Yehiel Michael Epstein understands it in the simplest terms. Citing Rabbi Caro verbatim and quoting earlier sources, he adds:

> And many have been mistaken in this and have said that a vocation is demeaning. Yet many talmudic sages were working men, and we have read in the Midrash that work is more dear than a distinguished lineage. . . . Still, one must never allow his work to be primary and his Torah to be temporary, but rather his Torah shall be primary and his work temporary, and thus both will be sustained.
>
> And it seems to me that this is only for a scholar whose main dealings are in Torah. But for an average householder this does not apply. For an average householder, there is no obligation other than to establish periods for study . . . [but a scholar] is obliged to study Torah all the day and all the night, except for what is necessary to seek his livelihood.[20]

Worthy of note is Rabbi Epstein's differentiation between the life's missions of the scholar, who must enforce Torah study as the core of his existence, and the householder, for whom there is no such obligation. Yet, even the scholar must take time from his studies to seek the material needs of his household. Elsewhere Rabbi Epstein argues that Maimonides himself would support a salary and financial emoluments for those whose wisdom and skill merit their appointment as communal functionaries and religious leaders. In effect, this has become their profession.

Though tangential to our discussion, Rabbi Epstein adds several interesting comments regarding honesty and integrity. Expanding Rabbi Caro's dictum that business dealings must be conducted faithfully, he adds that this cannot be an adjuration against theft or dishonest measures. Whether the victim is Jewish or Gentile, such evil was long ago condemned. Rather, faithful business dealings imply honesty in both word and deed. "Let his yes be true," Rabbi Epstein tells us.

The merchant is obliged to set honest value to his product, never lying even in the slightest. His dealings and negotiations should be relaxed, and he should not raise his voice in anger or in temper. From this his reputation as a pleasant and honest merchant will grow, redounding to the benefit of his business and generally facilitating his prosperity. Presumably, this advice applies to scholar and laymen alike as practitioners of a trade or vocation.[22]

However, Rabbi Yisrael Meir Ha-Kohen understood Rabbi Caro's ruling in favor of gainful employment quite differently. In his *Be'ur Halakhah* commentary,[23] he agrees that the workaday world is an appropriate venue for the large majority of otherwise pious and learned individuals. However, in each generation there are some few who stand on a spiritual and intellectual plane so exalted that they merit the right to devote themselves solely to Torah, depending upon the Lord for their material support and livelihood. His gloss evokes the words of the ancient sage Rabbi Shimon ben Yohai in the talmudic discourse from which much of this debate emerges.

Rabbi Yisrael Meir adds an important caveat, however. Even those who seek to attain this exalted plane may do so only if they find patrons and sponsors who agree in advance to support their exclusive commitment to Torah. To buttress his case, he adds a nuance not unknown but rarely invoked in earlier decisions and arguments surrounding this issue. He makes reference to a similar relationship said to have existed between Yissachar and Zevulun, sons of the biblical patriarch Jacob. The analogy has become a popular rallying point in the contemporary debate over this issue.[24]

A cursory glance at the text in which this famous relationship is rooted sheds light on our discussion. The rabbis appear troubled that in two separate biblical passages the tribes of Israel are enumerated out of their usual order. Both as they stand ready to receive Jacob's deathbed blessing and as they hear Moses' final charge, the elder, Yissachar, is listed only after Zevulun, the younger. The rabbis explain this as a function of the very unusual partnership carried on by these brothers and their families for many generations.

By prior arrangement, given the proximity of their territory to the Mediterranean coast, the descendants of Zevulun pursued commercial endeavors largely related to shipping and export. All the while, the families of Yissachar committed themselves exclusively to Torah study, supported by the profits and income earned by their cousins of Zevulun. Thus Yissachar was sustained materially while Zevulun was credited for a portion of the spiritual reward accrued by the Torah study he supported. Yet, the rabbis conclude, as a reflection of the relative importance they attribute to the success of this partnership, Scripture ignores their birth order and gives priority to Zevulun, the tradesman and merchant, over Yissachar the scholar. The point will be explored further below.

V

Recent rabbinic authorities have introduced nuances to the discussion rarely invoked previously, even by those who supported their respective positions. These have generally been marshaled on behalf of exclusive Torah study, the obligations of the public to support its proponents, and the sanction for scholars to accept support lest they be distracted from their studies.

Rabbi Yisrael Meir HaKohen once again provides us with an important example.[25] In addition to his analogy with the biblical partnership between Yissachar and Zevulun, he finds still another early model for today's scholars. He refers us to the tribe of Levi, whose members were set apart and exempted from certain civic obligations in order to perform various public and religious functions in ancient Israel. It was for them to demonstrate "the pathways of the Lord and His righteous justice to the masses" and to serve as "the army of God." In consequence they were not apportioned a geographic base but were dispersed in cities and religious centers throughout the country, to be supported by the tithes and taxes mandated in Scripture.

To make his case for the analogy between today's scholars and the ancient tribe of Levi, Rabbi Yisrael Meir cites the following from Maimonides' discussion of the Sabbatical and Jubilee years:

> And not just the tribe of Levi alone, but every individual from anywhere in the world whose spirit moves him, and by his wisdom he separates himself to stand before the Lord, to serve and to know God and walk honestly before Him. He shall relieve himself of the yoke of the many demands that people seek. Therefore is this one sanctified among the most

holy, and the Lord will be his portion and his heritage forever. He shall merit in this world that which is sufficient for himself, as did the Priests and the Levites.[26]

The reference is curious, however. A careful reading of Maimonides provides no indication that exclusive Torah study at public expense was the function of the Levites of old. In fact, it is nowhere mentioned in the chapter under discussion and flies in the face of his vituperation against such practices elsewhere. Moreover, none of the primary commentaries to his work, or subsequent scholars, for that matter, makes any such allusion. This includes Rabbi Yosef Caro, who, as we have amply demonstrated above, takes him to task on this very issue.

In fact, the point seems to have disturbed Rabbi Dovid ibn Zimri, who provides the sole relevant gloss on this passage. In his notes to Maimonides, he offers a meticulous reading of the phrase "he shall merit in this world that which is sufficient for himself." Then Rabbi Dovid adds, "The Holy One will enable him to profit from the world that which is sufficient for himself, and he shall not thrust himself on the public." This clearly runs quite contrary to the analogy being struck between the ancient men of Levi and those who seek to devote themselves exclusively to Torah study. At least in the mind of Rabbi Dovid ibn Zimri, Maimonides does not give license here for their public support.[27]

Rabbi Moshe Feinstein provides us with another recent spirited defense of Torah as an exclusive profession, in lengthy and far-ranging discourses published posthumous to his distinguished career.[28] Responding to petitions regarding secular and professional education and the commitment to Torah study, he strikes original ground, understanding and applying earlier sources in a unique and novel manner. For example, he takes great pains to demonstrate that it is not charity that changes hands in the relationship between Zevulun and Yissachar. To him, this is very much a formal business partnership in which each party benefits according to prior arrangements and understandings, much in the spirit of Rabbi Yisrael Meir's *Be'ur Halakhah* above.

Commenting about students whose skills may be insufficient to justify their exclusive devotion to Torah study, Rabbi Feinstein urges that they remain within the walls of the yeshiva all the same. If only by memory they still may master the great works of Talmud and its commentaries, a notable feat in itself. Ultimately, this will lead to deeper and more profound study. Moreover, one of questionable intellectual ability who enters a secular profession is liable to cause great damage and harm through his mistakes and misapprehensions. This is something "found quite often in medicine as a result of a lack of understanding and insufficient depth." If that occurs, he will have little option to call upon the Lord to aid in his success.

In considering the fundamental dispute between Rabbi Yishmael and Rabbi Shimon ben Yohai, Rabbi Feinstein argues that Rabbi Yishmael's apparent sanction to labor alongside Torah study was merely to work one's own fields. In this "they were engaged only for the days of Nissan [early spring] and the days of Tishrei [early autumn], and it was sufficient for the entire year," freeing them to devote themselves to study. His suggestion that Rabbi Yishmael's famous ruling should be understood so narrowly is unique and novel indeed.

Rabbi Feinstein summarizes his thinking succinctly.

> We consider no one a "child of the Torah" and a scholar except he who fulfills the obligation of Torah study properly

. . . that he will not distract his mind by other things or engage
in labor and business except for his survival. And if it is not
possible for him in this way, then he must be sustained by
charity. In our time, for hundreds of years we have given
license to serve as a rabbi for pay or as a lecturer in higher and
primary religious schools for pay, and he must accept such service.[29]

It bears note that in a much earlier ruling, obviously geared
to a lay public, the thrust of Rabbi Feinstein's thinking seems
to go otherwise. There, he claims that even those talmudic
sages who raise questions about the need to train one's child
for a trade (Kiddushin 82a–b) would agree that once past his
youth, "he must labor for his sustenance and for that of his
wife and children."[30]

Still another nuance inheres in the Jewish national renaissance that emerged with the advent of political Zionism and,
later, with the founding of the State of Israel. Now claims for
exclusive Torah study were pitted against yet another set of
religious obligations related to rebuilding the Holy Land. In
this, not only personal but also national considerations were
given vent. It may have been appropriate for large numbers of
scholars to commit themselves fully to their Torah studies during the long years of the Diaspora. No other vocation could
have provided the requisite spiritual fulfillment. Transplanted
to the ancestral homeland, however, and given the special mission of renewing it, alternative pathways for religious expression emerged. Each could contribute according to his talents.

Rabbi Moshe Sofer anticipated this line of thought early in
the nineteenth century. He argued that Rabbi Yishmael's
exhortation to work the fields in search of one's livelihood was
specific to the Land of Israel, whose development was a religious obligation in itself. Torah study could no more exempt
one from working to settle the land than from praying each

day. Nor could the people of God tolerate the embarrassment of foreigners serving in critical professional or vocational capacities throughout the country.[31] It is at least ironic that precisely in modern Israel do we find the largest number of young pietists committed to Torah study exclusively, claiming it as an alternative means to fulfill their civic obligations.

Finally, there are empirical data that provide a unique test of these issues among the working laity in contemporary Israel. The results take us full circle, evoking the sentiments with which we began this exploration. In a recent study of workplace attitudes, workers were asked:

> Imagine that you won a lottery or inherited a large sum of money and could live comfortably for the rest of your life without working; what would you do about work—continue or stop working? In Israel, only 10.3% of the non-religious respondents said they would stop working, whereas 21% of the respondents with strong religious convictions show such a desire. When the latter were asked, "Why would you stop working?" their overwhelmingly prevalent reply was "to practice and study the Torah."[32]

The broad majority of workers, whatever their religious sensibilities, report that should fortune smile upon them in this unexpected manner, they would continue on the job. Apparently work values remain central for them, despite their ideological or spiritual differences. It is revealing, however, that more than twice as many "with strong religious convictions" say that, like Tevye, if they were rich they would forego their work in favor of religious study and practice.

VI

A summary of our discussion must begin with a point that is both obvious and necessary. It has been our intent to explore the place of Torah study within the framework of work values. We have demonstrated that the mainstream of Jewish thought appears to favor a life of balance, certainly for the large majority of its adherents, and questions the legitimacy of those who would devote themselves exclusively to the study hall, depending upon public support for their sustenance. Yet none of this should be interpreted as an attack on Torah study. After all, most everything that has been marshaled here is rooted in its sources, indicating, if nothing else, that the question of balance and priority has occupied interpreters of the tradition for tens of centuries.

Alongside the texts and sources here provided there are counter-texts that may be construed to the contrary, a trait that has given vitality to Judaism and Jewish thought over the ages. Moreover, every culture and civilization makes special provision for its pietists and sages. Those committed to Torah study exclusively have always had a unique place reserved for them by the tradition. Under the limits and conditions described, the tradition suggests that modern Israel and Jewish communities elsewhere should be no different.

Yet that may be precisely the point. The mainstream of rabbinic thinking sharply differentiates the broad majority of the population and a small, select handful of scholars. The former expresses its religious devotion and fulfills its spiritual obligations in large measure by working diligently and honestly, setting aside time for study and reflection as possible. The commitment of the people in this segment of the populace to honest and gainful employment is in no wise demeaning, nor does it undermine their status among the faithful of the Lord.

By the same token, the study hall as an exclusive domain is reserved for the very few. Even those who have made a spirited defense of this lifestyle over the years would hardly argue that it was intended as normative and modal for the broad population. It is scarcely likely that they envisioned tens of thousands of students entering this pursuit virtually as an entitlement, with little consideration for their abilities or predisposition, and with little to hold them accountable.

Indeed, in the minds of leading authorities over the generations, even one who claims the "Torah as his profession" is obliged to earn his keep and see to the material needs of his family. He is warned not to depend upon charity for his maintenance, nor to "thrust himself upon the public." Aside from serving as a practical shield against poverty and the dole, this would also serve to safeguard and uphold Torah study. Consequently, numerous rabbinic opinions, codes, and formal rulings define a scholar as one who allows himself no distraction from study, save for the time and toil required to earn his livelihood.

Hardly a distraction, according to many, it is a mitzvah, a religious obligation which embodies intrinsic spiritual value. Whether directly or by implication, they made it clear that gainful employment never undermined one's claim to "Torah as his trade." Over this there was little debate.

The intellectual battle raged over the legitimacy of taking any financial benefit from Torah, whether in return for service as a teacher or religious leader, or as an outright grant in the pursuit of religious study. Even among those who supported the idea, it was seen as a concession. Latter-day scholars, they opined, simply could not earn their keep while attempting to master texts. To place this added burden upon their shoulders was a sure formula for the abandonment of Torah.

They agreed that the better part of piety and religious valor was to refuse public support, and those with the means were called upon to refrain from accepting it, even by many who found merit in the principle. It is a relatively recent claim that intensive Torah study is a contribution to communal well-being and security, evocative of the status of the ancient Levite, or that it qualifies per se for charitable support. Except to exempt themselves from local taxes and related levies, scholars rarely raised the issue.

In this vein, the words of Rabbi Yisrael Meir HaKohen, often invoked in support of exclusive Torah study at public expense, deserve one more look. First, his gloss to Rabbi Caro's ruling in favor of gainful employment is directed at the exclusive and exceptionally qualified few. It is hardly clear that he would countenance the emergence of communities, the bulk of whose male populace enters a life of full-time study by right, and whose female populace will marry no one that toils for his bread. Nor might he agree that they should raise their children to expect the same, or that their sustenance should be provided by involuntary taxpayers and unwitting philanthropists as a matter of public policy.

Moreover, he demands that even the exalted few who may merit the pristine existence of the rabbinic study hall seek out sponsors and patrons willing to underwrite their Torah study by prior arrangement, caring for the financial needs of their families on an individual and voluntary basis. Nowhere is life on the dole lauded or showcased as a model for the next generation. The midrash he cites, regarding the partnership between Yissachar and Zevulun, reinforces the point. Read carefully, it is no mandate for scholars to accept support as part of a service in which benefactors operating out of an obligation derive the greater benefit.

It must be recalled that Zevulun is given priority for his secular and material endeavors on behalf of pious Yissachar and his studies. Properly channeled employment and commercial pursuit are held aloft here. Alongside those few groomed for exclusive study, perhaps well-intentioned yeshiva students should be flocking to follow this other model, even as their instructors work diligently to develop a new generation of Zevuluns: highly successful business leaders and professionals with a special sensitivity for learning.

One practical consideration remains. The themes struck here may provide direction for contemporary public policy. In choosing a life of exclusive Torah study, young scholars in Israel may be seeking exemption from the armed services as much as from the workplace. Correctly or not, they fear that the substance and circumstances of military service will be damaging to their religious observance and personal piety. As a by-product of their exemption, however, they are legally proscribed from working, reminiscent of the medieval debate over tax exemptions for Jewish scholars. Under current legislation, to pursue a trade and earn income might mean their immediate conscription.

The Israeli military and its civilian overseers would be well advised to follow the mainstream precedent of Jewish thought and modify this stance. Concern for shirkers notwithstanding, by excluding sincere young scholars from job training and business experience, they are not likely to eliminate the manipulative few. Those who choose to malinger can access a substantial underground economy within which they may earn their keep sub rosa. Instead, the current policy merely ensures that the large majority of sincere students willing to pursue even a meager livelihood will be severely hampered and forced to depend upon the dole. The growing numbers who seek positions in acceptable trades and vocations after the age of thirty, the age at which their military eligibility expires, merely confirms the point.

In fact, small reflections of such change have recently emerged. At this writing, Israeli political leaders are reviewing the recommendations of the Tal Commission, empaneled in August 1999 in response to a Supreme Court ruling. The commission has called for a variety of alternatives to formal conscription that might allow haredi yeshiva students to fulfill their civic obligations and then enter the workforce by their mid-twenties. This includes deferring military eligibility to age twenty-four, four months of active duty at age twenty-six, followed by reserve status, or performing a year of civilian service in communal and charitable institutions. A move to lower the eligibility ceiling to age twenty-five is also being considered. Such changes are being matched by the creation of programs for higher education and job training exclusively designed for haredi men and women and operated under their auspices.

By the same token, opponents claim that such insular and segregated programs will further isolate the haredi community and reinforce their exclusion from meaningful economic and vocational endeavor. Moreover, continued special treatment creates an intolerable inequity, as non-haredim will still be expected to bear the brunt of civic obligation through years of military and reserve duty. The resultant backlash will do nothing to heal the social strains and will ultimately operate against haredim in the form of job discrimination and bias.

For their part, the haredi opposition condemns these recommendations as thinly veiled attempts to lure pious, saintly scholars out of the study hall and into a secular world of sin and corruption. Public protests have been mounted with calls for those involved to ignore the new initiatives and continue their studies in force. Clearly any such policies are tentative and will require fine-tuning and modification as they are implemented. Nevertheless, they represent the first small steps in a broad mission to reassert the balance between study and work values that stands at the core of classical Jewish thought.[33]

1. See also Rabbi Yosef Caro Beit Yosef: Orach Chaim 388:1 and Rabbi Moshe Maimonides, *Shelot U'Teshuvot Harambam*, item 123.

2. See, e.g. the exchange between Jonathan Rosenbloom and Moshe Korda in *The Jerusalem Post*, December 11, 1998 and December 14, 1998.

3. *Jerusalem Post* December 10, 1998.

4. See interview with General Yehuda Duvdevani, Commander of Youth, Nahal and National Missions, Ministry of Defense, *Jerusalem Post* January 7, 2000.

5. Bilha Mannheim and Avraham Sela, "Work Values in the Oral Torah" *Journal of Psychology and Judaism* 15 (4): 241–259 - Winter, 1991 - p. 252.

6. See *Tosafot: Brachot* 35b, s. v. *kan bizman she-Yisrael*, and Rabbi Shmuel Ideles, *Agadot Hamaharsha: Brachot* 35b, s. v. shene-emar.

7. See e.g. Rabbi Mordecai Greenberg, *Henaheg Bahem Minhag Derekh Eretz: Bayn Torah VeAvodah LeToratam Umnatam*, Yeshivat Kerem B'Yavneh, 1999; and Rabbi Ovadiah Yosef, *Shelot U'Teshuvot Yechaveh Daat*, 3:75. For a contrasting view, see Rabbi Moshe Feinstein, *Iggerot Moshe: Yoreh Deah* 4:36. It is worth noting that the juxtaposition of these two debate for purposes of clarifying the relationship between work and religious study was largely ignored by most thinkers until modern times. The most cogent observations emerge almost exclusively from rabbinic thinkers of the last centuries. For a full discussion of attempts, both early and recent, to reconcile the two texts, see Yeshuda Levi, *Torah Study: A Survey of Classic Sources on Timely Issues*. Jerusalem: Feldheim Publishers, 1990, especially pp.56–63.

8. Rabbi Ovadiah Bar Tenora, Avot 2:2 sv *vechol Torah*, *Rashi*, *Avot* 2:2 sv *Sheyegiat*, and *Lesof*, Rabbi Moshe Maimonides (Rambam) *Perush HaMishnayot: Avot* 2:2 and Rabbenu Yonah Gerondi *Avot* 2:2 sv *vechol Torah*.

9. Rabbi Moshe Maimonides (RAMBAM) *Yad HaHazakah: Hilchot Talmud Torah*, 3:10–11 and *Perush HaMishnayot: Avot* 4:5.

10. Rabbi Yosef Caro, *Kesef Mishneh Hilchot: Talmud Torah* 3:10.

11. Rabbi Shimon ben Tzemach Duran *Tashbetz*, 1:146.

12. *Shelot U'Teshivot HaRosh*, 15:10.

13. Rabbi Mordechai HaLevi, *Shelot U'Teshivot Darkhei Noam: Choshen Mishpat* item 55 and 56.

14. See e.g. Rabbi Yisrael Isserlein, *Terumat Hadeshen* item 342; Rabbi Moshe Al-Shakar, *Shelot U'Teshivot Maharam Al-Shakar*, item 19; Rabbi Benyamin ben Matityahu, *Shelot U'Teshivot Binyamin Zev*, item 252; Rabbi Levi Ben Yacov Ibn Haviv, *Shelot U'Teshivot Maharalbach*, item 140; *Sefer Kolbo* item 147. Also, see the rulings of Rabbi Yosef Caro *Sulchan Arukh: Yoreh Deah* 243:2 and Rabbi Shabbtai HaCohen, *Siftei Kohen: Yoreh Deah* 243:6–7.

15. Rabbi Yacov ben Asher Ba'al Haturim, *Tur Shulchan Arukh: Yoreh Deah*, 246, and *Orach Chaim*, 156; Rabbi Yosef Caro, *Beit Yosef: Yoreh Deah*, 246:21 and *Orach Chaim*, 156:1.

16. Rabbi Shabbtai HaCohen, *Siftei Kohen: Yoreh Deah*, 246:20.

17. Rabbi David ben Shmuel Halevi, *Turei Zahav: Yoreh Deah*, 246:21.

18. Rabbi Moshe Isserlies (REMA) *Yoreh Deah*, 246:21.

19. Rabbi Yosef Caro, *Shulhan Arukh: Orakh Hayyim* 151:1.

20. Rabbi Yechiel Michael Epstein, *Oreykh HaShulchan: Orach Chaim*, 156:1–2.

21. Rabbi Yechiel Michael Epstein, *Oreykh HaShulchan: Yoreh Deah*, 246:39.

22. Rabbi Yechiel Michael Epstein, *Oreykh HaShulchan: Orach Chaim*, 156:3.

23. Rabbi Yisrael Meyer Ha-Cohen, *Beur Halakha: Orach Chaim*, 156:1.

24. See e.g. *Bereshit Rabbah* 99, s.v. *zevulun le hof*.

25. Rabbi Yisrael Meyer Ha-Cohen, *Beur Halakha: Orach Chaim*, 156:1

26. Rabbi Moshe Maimonides (RAMBAM) *Yad HaHazakah: Hilchot Shemittah VeYovel* 13:13.

27. Rabbi Dovid Ibn Zimri (RIDVAZ) *Hilchot Shemittah VeYovel*, 13:12.

28. Rabbi Moshe Feinstein, *Iggerot Moshe: Yoreh Deah*, 4:36–37.

29. Rabbi Moshe Feinstein, *Iggerot Moshe: Yoreh Deah*, 4:36, p. 233.

30. Rabbi Moshe Feinstein, *Iggerot Moshe: Orach Chaim*, 3:111.

31. *Hiddushei Chatam Sofer: Sukkot* 36a; see also R. Ovadiah Yosef, *Yechaveh Daat* 3:75.

32. Itzhak Harpaz. A Cross National Comparison of Religious Conviction and the Meaning of Work. *Cross Cultural Research*, 32(2):143–170 1998. See also Itzhak Harpaz, *The Meaning of Work in Israel: Its Nature and Consequences*. New York: Praeger, 1990; B. Shamir, "Protestant Work Ethic, Work Involvement and the Psychological Impact of Unemployment" *Journal of Occupational Behavior* 1986 7:25–38.

33. See e.g. *Jerusalem Post* April 14, 2000.

5

The Employee as Corporate Stakeholder

I

Neoclassical economic theory posits a simple doctrine regarding the ethics of business organization. Those involved in the marketplace have a singular obligation to increase profits. With the advent of the corporation, the introduction of public investment, and the separation of ownership from management, this obligation is transferred to the operating officers of the firm. As agents of those who own stock, they hold a fiduciary responsibility to increase the value of their holdings and maximize profits, with little concern for the broader social consequences of their actions. Accountability is the sole province of corporate principals whose assessments are based in profitability and growth.

This perspective was clearly articulated by Milton Friedman, for whom the suggestion that managers have a broader social responsibility was nothing less than "subversive." The "business of business is business," he argued. Those

An earlier version of this paper was presented at the Orthodox Forum (New York, 1996). It appeared as "The Employee as Corporate Stakeholder: Exploring the Relationship Between Jewish Tradition and Contemporary Business Ethics" in Aaron Levine and Moses Pava (eds.), *Jewish Business Ethics: The Firm and Its Stakeholders*. Northvale N.J.: Jason Aronson, 1999.

who advocate a "social conscience" to provide employment, overcome discrimination, or avoid pollution "are preaching pure and unadulterated socialism," he concluded.[1]

Absent the ideological rhetoric, this indifference to the broad social implications of corporate action was confirmed by Robert Allen, former chairman of AT&T. In the wake of a decision to cut some forty thousand jobs, his company's stock rose by $7 per share. This increased corporate value by approximately $11 billion, and Allen's personal stock holdings and options by some $5 million. Responding to suspicious questions, Allen said:

> "Increasing shareholder value is the right incentive for me to have at AT&T. Is it the right incentive for me to affect 40,000 people? Hell, I don't know. . . . Is it fair? Hell, I don't know if it's fair. I don't make the rules."[2]

Notwithstanding, there is ample evidence to suggest that early-on, many corporate leaders sensed obligations to constituencies other than shareholders, if only as a modality for increased profit. Preston cites a Depression-era commitment by the General Electric Corporation to satisfy the needs of four major groups: shareholders, employees, customers, and the general public. So too, Robert Johnson, president of Johnson & Johnson in 1947, identified the company's primary clientele as customers, employees, managers, and stockholders. Robert Wood, CEO of Sears in 1950, argued that profit would best result from satisfying corporate responsibilities to employees, customers, and society at large.[3]

Such anecdotal evidence from captains of industry is confirmed by empirical studies of corporate leadership over the past three decades. Surveys of upper-level managers suggest that large majorities believe it unethical for corporations to ignore the needs of customers and employees in favor of stock-holders. In practice, they tend to identify their role as satisfying a broad clientele, including shareholders.[4]

R. Edward Freeman succinctly articulated this tendency and the moral basis that is its underpinning as "stakeholder theory." Building upon earlier work in the area of corporate social responsibility, governance, and performance, Freeman originated a systematic framework for assessing the roles of the multiple constituencies affected by corporate decisions, whose needs and interests must be accommodated in commercial policy and management strategy.[5] Over the past decade and a half, his framework has been elaborated and refined, subjected to deconstructionist analysis and feminist theory, reduced to a series of research propositions, and applied to policy concerns beyond the scope of business and commercial strategy.[6]

In a most fruitful attempt to distinguish stakeholder theory from other strains in the literature linking business, ethics, and society, Donaldson and Preston have identified alternative perspectives for its application: descriptive, instrumental, and normative.[7] In its first formulation, considering multiple constituencies is something managers do from an intuitive sense of fair play. They are encouraged by their legal and social operating context and by the faith that such considerations will support their strategic objectives. As such, stakeholder theory becomes a value-free description of managerial reality awaiting empirical confirmation.

On a second level, stakeholder theory is instrumental. It offers a route to effectively pursue commercial strategy. Here the essential mission of the corporation remains profitability and increased shareholder value. Attending the needs of other stakeholders, however, is a quick and efficient means of reaching these goals. It increases sales and helps hold costs down while reducing liability and the demand for external regulation.

Finally, normative principles sit at the core of stakeholder theory. Concern for the full scope of social interests represented by all those affected by managerial strategy is an ethical and moral obligation. This holds true regardless of whether it appears reasonable to corporate leadership or increases their profit. Managers are fiduciaries and agents to be sure, but they represent the interests of everyone on whom their decisions impact. They should be held accountable to this broad-based set of constituencies or to the public agencies that are their advocates.

Employees rank high in any assessment of those who may not hold corporate stock but are directly affected by managerial policy. Osigweh places them within the "internal environment" of commercial activity, alongside managers and shareholders, and closer to the heart of corporate organization than customers and suppliers.[8] Clarkson suggests that employees have many more concerns and are more frequently affected by corporate strategy than any other stakeholders. He counts no fewer than twenty such policy areas that have an impact on employees, at least twice as many as any other group. These range from compensation and benefits to unionization and collective action, from dismissals, layoffs, and appeals to occupational safety and health.[9]

What follows is an exploration of the classical Jewish texts and sources regarding the status of employees as "stakeholders" of the firm. We will consider the demands of Jewish tradition regarding their rights in selected areas, including the administration of pay and benefits, and occupational health and safety. The closing section will place these findings within the context of corporate stakeholder theory.

II

As we have seen, Jewish orientations regarding responsibility toward employees, or *po'alim*, derive from several sources: the status of work and the worker, the employment relationship, analogous legislation, especially that which regulates indentured servitude, and the presence of *minhag*, here defined as accepted business practice.[10] The best-known elements of an employer's responsibility to his workforce in the classical Jewish texts relate to compensation management and the distribution of pay. Scripture demands that every effort be made to pay workers punctually. Employers are warned that the wages of a hired servant "shall not abide with you until morning" (Leviticus 19:13). Equally, "you shall not oppress a hired servant who is poor and needy, whether he be of your brethren or of the strangers who are within your land and your gates. In his day shall you give him his hire, nor shall the sun go down upon it, for he is poor, and to it he sets his spirit; lest he cry to the Lord against you and it be a sin in you" (Deuteronomy 24:14–15).

The concern for timely payment is summarized under the general descriptor *lo talin*, after a phrase in the Hebrew text of Leviticus 19:13, the first reference cited above. With these as base, the Talmud and the Midrash declare, and Maimonides rules, that an employer who maliciously withholds payment may be liable for as many as five transgressions.[11] Wages are due within hours of the completion of a shift. For an employee whose workday ends after nightfall, this means before daybreak. For an overnight worker, this means before the following nightfall, whether it ends a day, a week, or even a year of hire.[12]

The reasoning that undergirds this stringent demand for

punctuality is twofold. The predominant rationale is a presumption of poverty grounded in the phrases "you shall not oppress a hired servant who is poor and needy" and "nor shall the sun go down upon it [his hire], for he is poor," cited above. Biblical commentary underscores the point. For example, Nahmanides explains that without his pay, an employee will scarcely be able to feed his hungry family that very night. "He is poor," Nahmanides concludes, "as are most who give themselves for hire." Similarly, the author of *Sefer ha-Hinnukh* notes that "all workers, or most, require their pay for their food. Therefore it is improper to delay to him his food, and in this vein it is written: 'for he is poor.'"[13]

Given a presumption of poverty, the demand for prompt payment of wages appears as a function of broader charitable impulses, beyond the context of the workplace. Consequently, it seems reasonable to relax employer liability in regard to more affluent employees. This eventuality is considered in the Talmud, though largely by implication. For example, in its analysis of biblical sources, such terms as "poor" and "needy" are understood to demonstrate that if an employer has insufficient funds to meet his entire payroll, needy workers have first claim. In principle, however, it appears that even wealthy employees can claim prompt payment under the provisions of *lo talin*. The point is elaborated explicitly in the Zohar, the primary source of Jewish mysticism.[14]

This forms a second prop to the scriptural mandate. Workers, even those who cannot demonstrate need, depend upon prompt payment nevertheless. It is toward that end that they extend themselves, often assuming personal risk while executing their tasks and responsibilities. In the language of the Talmud, "Why does he ascend upon a ladder, suspend himself from a tree, and place himself at risk of death [if] not for his wage? . . . One who withholds the pay of a worker, it is as if he takes his spirit from him."[15] Thus, apart from their subjective levels of need, employees have a claim to immediate pay that is rooted in the effort and the time invested in their jobs.

The point is amplified by a related talmudic discussion. There is little question that wages are due upon the completion of a shift. Still, at several junctures the rabbis carry on a lively, if somewhat abstract debate regarding the theoretical essence of pay. Rabbi Meir argues that the total wage is due upon the completion of a job; the Sages held that pay was cumulative, accruing with the completion of each intermediary task.

By their assessment, wages remain with the employer as a loan that comes due upon completion of the job. Most authorities confirm this position, though its implications are few and distant from current concerns. However, it may serve to reinforce the claim of an affluent employee. Loans must be repaid in a timely fashion, without regard to the financial status of the creditor. So too the financial status of a worker, a creditor of sorts in relation to his wage, is not relevant to the employer's liability in meeting his obligations punctually.[16]

In a related gesture on behalf of employees, Jewish tradition facilitates their claims in payroll disputes. Under normal circumstances, defendants in a civil case who make partial admission to the existence of a debt are required to take an oath against the remainder. In the original formulation, those who fully deny the debt's existence are free of any liability, though at a later point in talmudic history, a special oath was introduced for them as well. Disputes over pay, however, represent the first of a handful of instances in which the initiative is shifted to the claimant. Workers at the completion of a shift, whose hire is stipulated but who claim that they have yet to be paid, are permitted to take an oath to that effect and collect their due, no matter their employer's counter-claim.[17]

The Talmud debates the legal basis for this shift of initiative. Its instinct is to assign this innovation to the general tilt in favor of worker rights. In the words of Rabbi Nahman, the oath was "transferred to the worker because of his livelihood." An objection is raised regarding what amounts to a legal disadvantage for the employer, based on an abstract concern for the protection of wages. Numerous arguments are mounted to illustrate that the employer is so taken with his financial and commercial responsibilities that he implicitly concedes this initiative to protect his integrity and credibility with his workforce. The details of this lengthy discussion notwithstanding, most commentaries suggest that the Talmud remains true to its initial impulse. Whether the oath was instituted to substantiate fact or to set the mind of the employer at ease, its basis lies in a concern for the well-being of workers and the protection of their wages.[18]

However, both in meeting payrolls punctually and in confirming worker claims of non-payment, exemptions are provided to facilitate extenuating circumstances and to ensure that concern for the prerogatives of labor do not interfere unduly with the pursuit of normal enterprise. For example, if particular accounts-receivable must be settled before the regular payroll can be covered, an extension is automatically granted the employer as an implicit aspect of the employment contract. The same applies if the time required to complete wage calculations extends beyond the provisions of *lo talin*.

In cases where the employer has no available funds to cover the payroll, an extension also is provided, until such funds are available. At that point, employee claims precede those of other creditors. Several authorities suggest that an employer is at least morally obligated to dispose of other assets or to seek a loan elsewhere to cover his payroll and fulfill his commitments to his employees. Further, he would be wise to stipulate, as part of the original employment contract, that he will be held blameless, should fiscal circumstances conspire to prevent him from meeting his payroll.[19]

III

Severance pay is an interesting study in the application of the several sources for responsibility to employees in normative Jewish thought. Some have sought precedent for severance benefits in the requirement to provide *ha-anakah*, a gratuity or bonus to the indentured Hebrew, normally upon the completion of his six-year term of service. Thus, "and when you let him go free from you, you shall not let him go empty. You shall furnish him liberally of your flock and of your threshing-floor and of your winepress; of that which the Lord your God has blessed you, shall you give to him" (Deuteronomy 15:12–14).

The Talmud, its commentaries, and the authors of later codes record numerous debates about the details of this benefit.[20] Was it due any Hebrew servant or only those indentured by virtue of criminal guilt? Was it a philanthropic gesture on the part of the master, or an integral aspect of remuneration to the servant for additional services rendered during the term of indenture? Was it a flat-rate bonus or calculated pro rata to the prosperity enjoyed during the term of indenture?

These issues aside, the author of *Sefer ha-Hinnukh* strikes new ground in extending *ha-anakah* to workplace relations generally. He concedes that the institution of the Hebrew servant, along with most practices related to it, were all linked to the Jubilee year and, consequently, discontinued with the destruction of the Second Temple. Nevertheless, even at this time, "'let the wise one listen and add wisdom' (Proverbs 1:5). Should [he] hire one from among the children of Israel, and he work for him for a long time, or even a brief while, when he leaves him, let [the employer] give *ha-anakah* from that which the Lord has blessed him."[21]

While the analogy between the Hebrew servant and the employee is intriguing, most authorities do not find it compelling. As the language above suggests, it has been understood in largely moral rather than legal terms as a basis for employee benefits. In consequence, severance pay has also been rooted in the more general obligation for employers to deal compassionately with their workers, emerging from the precedent of Rabbah bar Hanan and his porters (Bava Metzia 83a) discussed at length elsewhere (pp. 25–30).

This has found modern expression in the thinking of Rabbi Ben-Zion Ouziel and was later invoked in an award of severance pay by the Rabbinical Court of Haifa to employees of Hinnukh Atzmai, Israel's independent parochial school system. Thus:

> It is the responsibility of the employer not to act harshly with his employees and managers but to the contrary, with a pleasant eye and open heart. He must fulfill "and guard the pathways of the righteous." The court has the power to attach funds from an employer on behalf of his workers in all instances that it deems within the context of "so that you walk the good road and guard the pathways of the righteous." It may do so according to its assessment of the status of the employer and of the workers, and the circumstances of the termination.[22]

Finally, employers have also been held liable for severance based on the existence of *minhag*; in other words, that such is a usual and customary labor practice. In this sense, the benefit accrues to the employee neither from a sense of moral obligation imposed by the court nor by analogy with a defunct institution, such as the Hebrew servant. Rather, it is implicit in the conditions of employment as part of prevailing business practice. In general, to be imbued with the legal power of *minhag*, a practice must be both "spread throughout all the lands" and "common and employed frequently."[23] Thus Rabbi Ouziel, cited above, was hesitant to base his aforementioned ruling on an extant *minhag* of severance benefits to workers. To his mind, "the practice has not yet been accepted throughout the land, and it is not common, save for specific circumstances."

However, in his treatment of the issue some years later, Rabbi Eliezer Waldenberg found sufficient cause to conclude that a *minhag* had developed along these lines, and he stood ready to employ it in his ruling. He notes the moral precedent implicit in *ha-anakah* for a Hebrew servant and even enters the debate over the details of its implementation. Yet his finding was based upon contemporary labor practices rather than ancient precedent, even to the size of the benefit due the petitioner. In his words:

> there exists a general *minhag* in the country to pay severance benefits to workers and managers of various categories, in the form of one month['s pay] for each year of service, by the most recent annual salary rate. . . . This has been rooted in the country for decades, with no distinction between full-time and part-time workers. Therefore it certainly was with this in mind that [the employer] engaged the petitioner.[24]

IV

Aside from wages, Jewish tradition also concerns itself with the various benefits to which workers may be entitled as a condition of their employment. Perhaps best known is the worker's right to eat of the produce of any field in which he is currently occupied. Thus

> When you shall enter the vineyard of your fellow, you may eat grapes until you are content in your spirit, but you shall not put any in your vessel. When you shall enter the standing corn of your fellow, then you may pluck the ears with your hand, but you shall not move a sickle to his standing corn.
> (Deuteronomy 23:25-26)

There is no reference to an employee here, and one source unsuccessfully attempted to infer a general license for visitors in a field to help themselves. However, the Talmud concludes that the biblical intent is to allow field hands to eat of their master's crop. Such benefits are provided even to the beast of burden (Deuteronomy 25:4). It would be cruel and unnatural to expect workers to harvest produce without enjoying some of the yield. Beyond that, such a restriction would only serve to encourage theft.

Consequently, the right is limited to agricultural workers involved in harvesting fresh produce and vegetation at the time of their shift, and it is not transferable to family members. Further, while there is no formal limit to the amount or the value they may consume, workers are warned not to abuse this privilege, lest their maintenance outweigh their labor and their service not be renewed.[25]

Such applications appear far afield to a discussion of employer responsibilities, especially in non-agrarian concerns.

Nevertheless, they may have keen application, if only in the breach. Apparently, aside from this example, Jewish tradition does not require employers to provide food, per diem maintenance, or related expenses unless doing so is stipulated in the original employment contract or as a customary adjunct to the employee's wage. In this way, benefits to the worker differ from those provided to an indentured Hebrew.

For the latter, the Talmud understands the biblical text "for [the servant's life] is good with you" (Leviticus 25:40) to mean that a householder is expected to provide support for both the Hebrew servant and his family. However, in the words of one commentary, it appears that "this is specifically for a Hebrew slave, who, in the verse, is set free after six [years]. For a worker for a year, a month, a week, or a day, we do not say this, as it is said in [Bava Metzia 83a], 'everything goes by local custom.'"[26]

Similarly, employees are not entitled to recompense for travel, living expenses, or per diem maintenance unless it is stipulated in advance or reimbursement is already a generally accepted employment practice. This derives from the adjudication of several disputes involving sales representatives, business agents, and even partners to a transaction in which no provisions were made for these expenses. In each case, the rulings suggest that, absent customary procedure to the contrary, the employee is entitled only to the salary agreed upon. Where such practice is customary, it appears that *minhag* also will dictate the normal per diem rate to which employees are entitled even if their actual expenses are lower.[27]

However, an employer may be found liable for costs above those normally related to the execution of the task. Particular concern is attached to the extreme and emergency circumstances related to the perils of travel in foreign lands.

Employers are expected to cover costs and damages that result from greater risk and exposure than an employee might normally be expected to assume. Noteworthy examples include imprisonment for trade in contraband, suits related to product liability, and a variety of taxes.[28]

Custom also weighs heavily on liabilities for work-related injuries. Of course employers are expected to maintain a safe and secure workplace, even as shopkeepers protect the safety of their customers and householders make their homes secure for visitors, "that you bring not blood upon it" (Deuteronomy 22:8). Beyond that, however, workers who suffer damages due to the normal execution of their task are not due compensation, their risk being a presumption of the job. Thus

> "it is written, 'and to [his wage] he sets his spirit' (Deuteronomy 24:15). We derive that for his wage does he scale a wall or suspend himself from a tree, [and] this means that occasionally he may fall and be killed. He has put himself at risk for his pay."[29]

Only when the negligence of an employer contributes to worker injury will a claim for compensation be considered, and once again, negligence is determined by deviation from customary employment practice. For an example, the talmudic sage Samkhus records in the name of Rabbi Meir that a porter injured on the job may claim compensation if his burden was one *kab* heavier than customary. Since the talmudic norm for such labor is thirty *kab*, it is inferred that employers are held negligent for injury resulting from a workload increase of one-thirtieth. At the same time, employees are held partially responsible for not objecting to the increased burden, and consequently may be compensated only for damages, but not for related benefits normally included in such suits.[30]

V

There can be little doubt that Jewish thought places a clear obligation upon an employer to consider the needs of his workforce. Regarding a host of benefits in the administration of the payroll, severance, and occupational safety, as well as certain fringe benefits, employers must be mindful of their obligations to labor. They will be held liable and accountable in the breach.

However, normative Jewish sources exhibit an equally clear intent to provide balance in employee relations, thereby helping to secure the pursuit of commercial interests. For example, exemptions are available to employers who are temporarily constrained from fulfilling scriptural demands regarding payroll. Similarly, beyond the basic requirements of workplace safety, workers are expected to take responsibility for their own health and security. Those who incur expenses or damages in the normal execution of their jobs may not be entitled to reimbursement. Jewish texts also oblige employees to work to their fullest capacity, lest they be guilty of theft in accepting wages for less than an honest effort.[31]

Nevertheless, there is an evident tilt in favor of workers, as shown by the creation of a special oath for them in support of disputed claims or by the declaration of an obligation to treat them with compassion. On the assumption of their poverty and vulnerability, workers are ceded special standing relative to their employers. There is much in common with stakeholder theory in that Jewish tradition appreciates a responsibility toward those affected by managerial decisions, employees most immediately, beyond the interests of profit.

Yet the parallels are limited and imperfect. Stakeholder theory presumes the autonomy of the business enterprise, separate and apart from its commitment to the broader social milieu. For this reason, responsibility to other constituencies can be perceived as little more than an instrumental strategy ultimately focused on profit—the carrot rather than the stick. By contrast, Jewish values perceive society as a corporate entity. Business pursuits and industrial strategies are but one element in a web of relationships that conform to a more general sense of human obligation and responsibility.

The point bespeaks important conceptual lacunae. Mired in a tradition of self-conscious commercial autonomy, students of business in most market economies must struggle to justify social responsibility. Seeking a moral "hook" upon which to hang the obligations of business to society, they often stretch the nature of commercial relations, turning the firm into a charitable institution or an instrument of social policy and placing the onus of responsibility completely upon its shoulders.

Moreover, they often ignore the possibility that managers may function as independent, assertive stakeholders rather than neutral, objective agents of profit and corporate success. Yet there is evidence to suggest that managers too pursue selfish concerns, attempting to increase their own discretion, often with arrogant indifference not only to the needs of multiple constituencies, but even to the narrow interests of their own shareholders.

Consider the governance movement and the various shareholder revolts it has engendered in Fortune 500 corporations over the past two decades. These revolts do not focus on increasing influence over management policy for stakeholders whose concerns may be legitimate but essentially tangential to the commercial objectives of the firm. Rather, they are intended to foster responsiveness to the needs of the very shareholders toward whom management owes a fiduciary responsibility.

Most recently, large investors, notably public and union-based pension funds, have demanded greater accountability from managers and board members. Their agenda includes a move to link executive compensation to corporate performance. The movement has also spread to smaller companies whose corporate leaders have been similarly indifferent. Apparently, stockholders require protection no less than stakeholders.[32]

In this vein, it is instructive to consider an oft-noted stylistic and substantive contrast between Western and Jewish ethical thought. The former is defined by its emphasis upon individual rights both enumerated and reserved. Here the individual, and by extension for our purposes the corporation, is legally and morally sovereign and has a primary claim to unrestricted liberty and discretion. It is public regulation that bears the burden of moral justification in an ethical arena that is inherently adversarial. Those who seek to regulate must foster the proposition that sits at the heart of this discussion, that the corporation and those who sit at its helm have a responsibility that extends beyond their profit statements.

Normative Jewish tradition, in contrast, presupposes obligation and accountability to a larger social or moral fabric. Thus indenture is discouraged because freedom is the natural human condition; yet one remains free to be a servant of the Lord. Similarly, a healthy respect for private property and initiative is evident, but management and ownership bear conservatory and custodial responsibilities within a complex web of relationships, ordained and cemented from above. The tradition venerates neither a struggle for individual freedom nor an inherent individual sovereignty, both of which contribute to the adversarial flavor of American political, legal, and economic culture. As a result, no moral battle can be waged over responsibility to the employee. The issues are operational and logistic. They concern adjudicating equity where the obligation to a network of multiple constituencies is already presumed.[33]

This leads to yet another important distinction. Stakeholder theory attempts to create a systematic conceptual base to respond to what has been the norm in Western culture and is now being restated as "neoclassical" economics. In that respect, its objectives are laudable and its mission profound. Jewish tradition, on the other hand, is precisely that, a tradition. It has emerged through millennia of practice, and its values often must be inferred from a host of varying sources. At least in the social and economic realm, it displays a commitment to evolutionary change in response to secular usage and local custom.

The thrust of arguments favoring obligations to the workforce remains consistent. Yet specific manifestations are not always equally rooted in the sources of Jewish tradition. Some, such as the punctuality of pay, are plainly stated in Scripture. They are the most obviously authoritative, emerging as they do from the earliest and purest Jewish expressions of social equity and the ethics of the workplace. Others derive from analogous social relationships, as between master and indentured servant. These cannot command the same authority; the analogies are imperfect, and the institutions from which they derive are obsolete. Still others emerge from a call to generosity and compassion toward those more vulnerable. Though morally commendable, the legal status of such principles has been called in question by numerous Jewish thinkers.

Finally, and most to the point, many are borrowed from what is customary and usual in contemporary business practice. They have little claim as characteristically Jewish formulations, excepting that when an insistence upon fastidious application would hamper the free flow of economic intercourse, the tradition will generally stand aside and incorporate local usage. Secular advances in responsibility to the workforce are thus automatically appended to the body of Jewish tradition, though a pure and original linkage is difficult to establish beyond the commitment to facilitate social and economic routine.

Herein resides one more caveat in the linkage between our two models. Langtry takes Freeman and his colleagues to task for assuming a unitary view of their theoretical foil, Milton Friedman and his neoclassical corporation. By their own admission, business leaders and executives express a moral and practical concern for the needs of multiple clienteles. Langtry calls this "tinged stakeholder theory." The primary responsibility of the firm is still to those who own its stock. However, this obligation must operate "subject not only to legal constraints but also to moral or social obligations. These might be, for example, grounded in moral rights possessed by people generally or by specific categories of people such as employees of the firm; or there might be moral duties of beneficence not grounded in rights of the recipients."[34]

Goodpaster makes a similar point. A firm may have a compelling responsibility toward multiple constituencies whose well-being is affected by its decisions. However, these remain "non-fiduciary." To expect corporate executives to act with equanimity toward all who hold a stake in their decisions robs the fiduciary relationship of its moral power and turns the modern private corporation into a public institution.[35]

Perhaps this summarizes our review of the Jewish sources regarding employee relations. Clearly, they favor a concern for and an obligation to the needs of the workforce. This is variously grounded in economic need, inequities of status, investment and risk on behalf of the job, general compassion, and a concern for those more vulnerable. In the ultimate case, it is rooted in an obligation to fulfill the word of God.

Still, this not nearly the same as positing a fiduciary responsibility to protect the interests of such stakeholders as a responsibility equal to or beyond the pursuit of profit and gain. To suggest that the same moral force resides there as in relationships with corporate principals is to misunderstand that which drives both models.

1. Milton Friedman, "The Social Responsibility of Business Is to Increase Its Profits," *New York Times Magazine*, September 13, 1970; see also idem, *Capitalism and Freedom* (Chicago: University of Chicago Press, 1962); J. C. Shepard, *The Law of Fiduciaries* (Toronto: Carswell, 1981); Oscar Williamson, *The Law of Discretionary Behavior* (London: Kershaw, 1965).

2. Quoted in Allan Sloan, "For Whom the Bell Tolls," *Newsweek*, January 15, 1996, p. 37.

3. Lee E. Preston and H. J. Sapeinza, "Stakeholder Management and Corporate Performance," *Journal of Behavioral Economics* 19, no. 4 (1990): 361–375; J. C. Worthy, *Shaping an American Institution: Robert E. Wood and Sears, Roebuck* (Urbana: University of Illinois Press, 1984).

4. See, e.g., Richard Baumhart, *An Honest Profit: What Businessmen Say About Ethics in Business* (New York: Holt, Rinehart & Winston, 1986); B. Z. Posner and William H. Schmidt, "Values and the American Manager," *California Management Review* 26, no. 3 (1984): 202–216.

5. R. Edward Freeman, *Strategic Management: A Stakeholder Approach* (Boston: Pitman, 1984); R. Edward Freeman and D. L. Reed, "Stockholders and Stakeholder: A New Perspective on Corporate

Governance," *California Management Review* 25, no. 3 (1983): 88–106; R. Edward Freeman and D. R. Gilbert, "Managing Stakeholder Relationships," in S. P. Sethi and C. M. Falbe, eds., *Business and Society* (Lexington: Lexington Books, 1987); William Evan and R. Edward Freeman, "A Stakeholder Theory of the Modern Corporation: Kantian Economics," in Tom Beauchamp and Norman Bowie, eds., *Ethical Theory and Business* (Englewood Cliffs, N.J.: Prentice-Hall, 1988); R. Edward Freeman and William Evan, "Corporate Governance: A Stakeholder Interpretation," *Journal of Behavioral Economics* 10, no. 4 (1990): 337–359; R. Edward Freeman, "The Politics of Stakeholder Theory: Some Future Directions," *Business Ethics Quarterly* 4, no. 4 (1994): 409–421.

6. See, e.g., Thomas M. Jones et al., "The Toronto Conference: Reflections on Stakeholder Theory," *Business and Society* 33, no. 1 (1994): 82–131; Bruce Langtry, "Stakeholders and the Moral Responsibility of Business," *Business Ethics Quarterly* 4, no. 4 (1994): 431–443; Andrew Wicks et al., "A Feminist Reinterpretation of the Stakeholder Concept," *Business Ethics Quarterly* 4, no. 4 (1994): 475–497; Thomas M. Jones, "Instrumental Stakeholder Theory: A Synthesis of Ethics and Economics," *Academy of Management Review* 20, no. 2 (1995): 404–437; John Altman, "Toward a Stakeholder-Based Policy Process," *Policy Sciences* 27, no. 1 (1994): 37–51; Robert A. Reineke, "Stakeholder Involvement in Evaluation: Suggestions for Practice," *Evaluation Practice* 12, no. 1 (1991): 39–44.

7. Thomas Donaldson and Lee E. Preston, "The Stakeholder Theory of the Corporation: Concepts, Evidence and Implications," *Academy of Management Review* 20, no. 1 (1995): 65–91.

8. C. A. B. Osigweh, "A Stakeholder Perspective of Employee Responsibilities and Rights," *Employee Responsibilities and Rights Journal* 7, no. 4 (1994): 279–296; also idem, "Toward an Employee Rights and Responsibilities Paradigm," *Human Relations* 43, 12 (1991): 1277–1309; idem, "Elements of an Employee Rights and Responsibilities Paradigm," *Journal of Management* 16, no. 4 (1990): 835–850.

9. Max Clarkson, "A Stakeholder Framework for Analyzing and Evaluating Corporate Social Performance," *Academy of Management Review* 20, no. 1 (1995): 92–117.

10. Normative Jewish texts recognize two categories of workers: *kablanim*, roughly equivalent to independent contractors, and *po'alim*, analogous to full-time employees. Important legal principles are derived from the distinction, as in Rabbi Yaakov Ba'al ha-Turim, *Tur Shulhan Arukh*, Hoshen Mishpat 333:2. By contrast, some of the literature cited here makes no such distinctions. It should be understood, therefore, that the focus of this exploration is upon the *po'el* as the closest analogy to the corporate employee considered in stakeholder theory.

11. Bava Metzia 110–111; Sifre, Ki Teze 145; Rabbi Moshe Maimonides, *Yad*, Hilkhot Sekhirut 11:2.

12. Rabbi Moshe Maimonides, *Yad*, loc. cit.; Rabbi Yaakov Ba'al ha-Turim, *Tur*, Hoshen Mishpat 339:1–4; Rabbi Yosef Caro, *Shulhan Arukh*, Hoshen Mishpat 339:1–3.

13. Rabbi Moshe ben Nahman, commentary to Deuteronomy 24:15; *Sefer ha-Hinnukh* 588.

14. Bava Metzia 111b; Zohar, Kedoshim 29:86; also see Rabbi Menahem ben Shelomoh Me'iri (1965), *Beit ha-Behirah*, Bava Metzia 111a. There, support is marshaled from the biblical phrase "to it [his wages] he sets his spirit."

15. Bava Metzia 112a.

16. Bava Kamma 99a, Kiddushin 48a, Avodah Zarah 19b. For its applications, see Rabbi Moshe Maimonides, *Yad*, Hilkhot Ishut 5:19–2; Rabbi Yosef Caro, *Shulhan Arukh*, Even ha-Ezer 38:13.

17. Shavuot 44–46. Regarding *shevuat heset*, the additional oath, see, e.g., Tosafot to Shavuot 45a, s.v. *ikruha rabbanan*.

18. See Shevuot 45b and commentary thereto of Rabbi Yitzhak Alfasi, Rabbi Nissim Gerondi, s.v. *ikruha*, and Rabbi Asher ben Yehiel; also Rabbi Moshe Maimonides, *Yad*, Hilkhot Sekhirut 11:6; Rabbi Yehiel Epstein, *Oreykh ha-Shulhan*, Hoshen Mishpat 89:2.

19. Bava Metzia 111–112; Rabbi Moshe Maimonides, *Yad*, Hilkhot Sekhirut 11:4; *Tur*, Hoshen Mishpat 339:8–9, *Beit Yosef*, s.v. *sakhir*; Rabbi Yosef Caro, *Shulhan Arukh*, Hoshen Mishpat 339:9–10; Rabbi Moshe Isserles, Hoshen Mishpat 339:10; Rabbi Avraham Eisenstadt, *Pithei Teshuvah* 339:8.

20. Kiddushin 14–15; Tosafot, s.v. *ve-iydakh*; Rabbi Moshe Maimonides, *Yad*, Hilkhot Avadim 3:12; Rabbi Shabbetai HaKohen,

Hoshen Mishpat 86:3; Rabbi Yehoshua Falk-Katz, Sefer Meire: Enayim; Hoshen Mishpat 86:2; Me'iri, Kiddushin 15a; Rabbi Shelomoh Zevin, ed., *Encyclopedia Talmudit* (Jerusalem: Yad ha-Rav Herzog, 1971), 9:774–787, s.v. "Ha-anakah."

21. *Sefer ha-Hinnukh* 483.

22. Rabbi Ben-Zion Ouziel, *Mishpatei Ouziel* 41 (Tel Aviv: Bezalel); cited in Rabbi Moshe Findling, *Te-Hukkat ha-Avodah* (Jerusalem: Schreiber, 1941), p. 133; see *Lev vs. Hinnukh Atzmai Council of Kfar Ata,* in *Piskei Din Rabaniyim* 3:95.

23. Rabbi Moshe Maimonides, *Yad*, Hilkhot Ishut 23:12; Rabbi Moshe Isserles, Hoshen Mishpat 331:1. Based on a ruling of the Rivash, Shillem Wahrhaftig adds that a *minhag* must be public knowledge and clear. Rema cites the opinion, though this element is excluded. Clearly, the full-time status of the employee is crucial in this and many other areas under discussion here. While our emphasis throughout this volume has been upon the *po'el,* or full-time employee, rather than the *kablan,* or private contractor, the interested reader should consult J. David Bleich, *Contemporary Halachic Problems* (New York: Yeshiva University Press, 1977), pp. 132–134, for a fuller consideration of the differences between them in regard to severance benefits.

24. Rabbi Eliezer Waldenberg, *Ziz Eliezer* 7:48, no. 10.

25. Bava Metzia 92a; Talmud Yerushalmi, Ma'asrot 82:6–7; Rabbi Moshe Maimonides, *Yad*, Hilkhot Sekhirut 12:1-3,11–13; Rabbi Yaakov Ba'al ha-Turim, *Tur*, Hoshen Mishpat 337:13,12,17.

26. Kiddushin 22a; and commentary of Rabbi Asher ben Yehiel thereto.

27. See Rabbi Samuel ben Adret, *She'elot u-Teshuvot Rashba* 3:140; Rabbi Ya'ir Bachrach, *Havvot Ya'ir* 154; Rabbi Yisrael Isserlein, *Terumat ha-Deshen* 323.

28. See Rabbi Moshe Trani, *She'elot u-Teshuvot Mabit* 3:156, 188; Rabbi Yosef Colon, *She'elot u-Teshuvot Maharik* 153; Rabbi Mordekhai ben Hillel, *Mordecai*, Bava Metzia 359. While there may be no formal claim to compensation, in case of an employee's death while on the job many authorities required compensation to the heirs of the deceased as a form of penitence for the employer, even if no negligence was involved. See, e.g., Rabbi Yaakov Weil, *She'elot u-Teshuvot*

Maharyoh 125; Rabbi Shmuel Medina, *She'elot u-Teshuvot Maharashdam* 435.

29. Rabbi Moshe ben Nahman, *Teshuvot ha-Rashba ha-Meyuhasot la-Ramban* 20. Regarding the responsibilities of a householder or a shop-keeper for the safety of visitors and clients, see Bava Kamma 16b, 32a–b; Rabbi Moshe Maimonides, *Yad*, Hilkhot, *Roze'ah u-Shemirat ha-Nefesh;* 11:4 and Nizkei Mammon 10:11.

30. Tosefta Bava Metzia 7:10; Bava Metzia 80b; Rabbi Moshe Maimonides, *Yad*, Hilkhot Sekhirut 4:7; Rabbi Moshe Halevi, cited in Rabbi Yaakov Ba'al ha-Turim, *Tur*, Hoshen Mishpat 308:8; Rabbi Yosef Caro, *Shulhan Arukh*, Hoshen Mishpat 308:7; and the commen-taries thereto of Rabbi Yehoshua Falk-Katz, Sefer Meirei Eynayim, 308:12; Rabbi Yaakov of Lissa, *Netivot Mishpat* 308:3; and Rabbi Aryeh Leib, *Kezot ha-Hoshen* 308:2.

31. Rabbi Moshe Maimonides, *Yad*, Hilkhot Sekhirut 13:7. See pp. 30–33.

32. *New York Times*, February 6, 1996, D:1, 8.

33. See, e.g., Robert Cover, "Obligation: A Jewish Jurisprudence of the Social Order," *Journal of Law and Religion* 5 (1987): 65–90; Steven Friedell, "The Different Voice in Jewish Law: Some Parallels to a Feminist Jurisprudence," *Indiana Law Journal* 67 (1992): 915–949; Aaron Schreiber, *Jewish Law and Decision Making: A Study Through Time* (Philadelphia: Temple University, 1979); Suzanne Stone, "In Pursuit of the Counter Text: The Turn to the Jewish Legal Model in Contemporary American Legal Theory," *Harvard Law Review* 106: 813–894.

34. Bruce Langtry, "Stakeholders and the Moral Responsibilities of Business," *Business Ethics Quarterly* 4 (1994): 431–443.

35. Kenneth Goodpaster, "Business Ethics and Stakeholder Analysis," *Business Ethics Quarterly* 1 (1991): 61–70.

6

By the Light of Halakhah
Multiple Employment and Jewish Law

I

Recent government statistics suggest that over 7.8 million American workers currently hold more than one regular job, with some estimates placing the number closer to 8.5 million. Known variously as moonlighting, supplementary employment, or multiple job-holding, this includes members of the workforce who hold primary jobs, generally full-time, while supplementing their incomes with full- or part-time employment after-hours. Similar trends are evident in other industrial economies, with marked increases in supplemental employment noted in Canada, Sweden, and Norway. Unlike the United States, there was a greater tendency for Canadian and European workers to hold several part-time jobs, with no full-time commitment to a primary employer.[1]

Although they constitute only about one in twenty workers in the United States, the presence of workers with more than one job has increased sharply over the past two decades. For example, in 1975 only 4.7 percent of all workers held more

An earlier version of this paper appeared in the *Torah U'Maadah Journal* 4 (1993): 175–186.

than one job. By 1985 this had increased to 5.4 percent, and according to new surveys conducted by the U.S. Department of Labor, by 1989 the rate had risen to 6.2 percent and remained constant as of 1996. Significantly, the percentage of female workers who engaged in moonlighting in 1975 was only 2.9 percent. The figure more than doubled to 5.9 percent in 1989 and rose to almost 6.3 percent in 1996.

The data reflect several socioeconomic factors. Almost half of those surveyed indicated that they indulged in moonlighting to meet regular household expenses and pay off current debt. The highest rates were recorded among white married males between thirty-five and forty-four years of age, followed closely by those between forty-five and fifty-four. These men were also far more likely to start independent businesses as their second jobs, especially in sales.

Further, the findings reflect increases in the percentage of women in the workforce, especially single heads of households unable to subsist on one salary alone. Indeed, of all women, the rate of multiple job holding was highest among those who were single, widowed, divorced, or separated, especially in their twenties. About two-thirds of these women indicated that this was their means of meeting regular household expenses and current debt.[2]

Finally, the greatest increases were a function of the expanding economy of the late 1980s, during which time skilled and professional labor was in sharp demand. This allowed industry to take advantage of an abundance of employees who made themselves available after hours. Workers employed in public administration, service industries, and education were among the most likely to moonlight, with university professors especially notable. The high rates in these areas probably reflect greater control over scheduling and possession of skills transferable within and across industry bounds.[3] The increase in moonlighting poses a series of dilemmas for the large organizations that are the primary employers of the workers involved, and a lively debate has emerged that crosses disciplinary lines. As expected, advocates are found on both sides of the question.[4]

The most obvious managerial concern pertains to whether moonlighting employees maintain the requisite level of quality, productivity, and performance at their "day jobs" despite their responsibilities elsewhere. Employers have a right to expect workers to present themselves in a proper condition and that their energies will not be sapped by activity external to the job. The point bespeaks physical readiness, as well as emotional stability and motivation.

More subtle concerns relate to potential conflicts of interest, competition, and client/customer "raiding." Employers worry that multiple job-holding may compromise the integrity of the service they provide because their employees have personal interests outside the organization. While this is a consideration no matter what the employment status of the worker, having a second job increases the potential.

Similarly, workers who have a second job in the same industry after hours may be in direct competition with their primary employers. This occurs whether they are self-employed or, worse yet, work for a competitor. It includes access to clients, proprietary information, and support personnel, making the problem still more acute. The temptation to "make business" for oneself, that is, to attract clients away or to suggest that they be in direct contact for future services, may be more than any employer can bear. Indeed, some managers even report that pilferage of supplies and equipment increases when employees moonlight.[5]

Finally, an argument is made against moonlighting on broader social grounds, based on the claim that supplementary employment frequently heralds an entree into the underground economy. Moonlighters may not report their second income to the government or may indulge in questionable practices to reduce their tax liabilities. In addition, they remove jobs from the market when they moonlight, depriving others who are still in search of primary employment.[6]

Consequently, employers claim that multiple jobholding by their employees should take place only at the sole discretion of the former, on a case-by-case basis. At the very least, they should be consulted before a worker decides to accept a job elsewhere. Determinations should be made in the context of the worker's performance record, the type of work to be accepted, and the needs of the primary employer. Finally, employers should retain the right to rescind the agreement if circumstances change or prove untenable.

By contrast, a substantial case has been made in favor of multiple employment. Advocates argue that it is a means of retaining and satisfying talented workers when an employer cannot continue to raise salary or benefits. But for moonlighting, they suggest, these employees would leave for other, more attractive positions elsewhere.

In addition, moonlighting employees gain valuable experience and learn important skills that they can utilize at their primary places of employment. It helps satisfy their need for challenge, personal growth, and relief from the tedium of the daily job routine. Concerns for proprietary access run in both directions. Ultimately, they may cancel each other and net gains for the primary employer.

In broader social terms, the jobs that moonlighters take are largely in their own private businesses or in situations that would not suffice as full-time employment. Consequently, they are not removing opportunities from the unemployed, who generally do not qualify for the specialized work involved. On the contrary, they are helping to fill an important need in organizations that could not otherwise afford to hire new personnel.

Finally, the nature of primary employment commits a worker to a given number of hours per week, prearranged by formal contract, letter of appointment, and industry practice. Despite the benefits or costs that may accrue, what workers do on their own time is outside the purview of the employer. They should have the right to exercise that option without managerial interference.[7]

II

What follows is an analysis of multiple employment from the perspective of halakhah and classical Jewish sources as they reflect upon employee relations generally. Concern about multiple employment dates to antiquity and was sufficiently acute to merit inclusion in several realms of talmudic discourse. Unlike most aspects of labor relations in Jewish thought, the early rulings in this sphere favor the employer's position on the question. For example, several talmudic references suggest that employees have a responsibility to perform efficiently on the job. Among other considerations, this includes a proscription against working after hours. Consider the following:

> A worker is not permitted to fulfill his own responsibilities by night so that he can hire himself by day. Nor may he plow with his ox by night and then lease her by day. Nor should he starve and thirst himself to feed his family, for this constitutes

theft of the employer's work. He will sap his strength and weaken his mind, and not do his work energetically.

(Tosefta Bava Metzia 8:2;
see also Talmud Yerushalmi, Demai 7:3)

Both the language and the context of this passage reflect a commitment to full personal productivity. Anything that reduces the worker's performance is disallowed. This means that he must take care of his mental and physical health, making sure to eat and rest properly. After-hours employment is a likely impediment to productivity and therefore prohibited. Numerous medieval authorities cite this ruling of the Tosefta as binding, among them Rabbi Yitzhak Alfasi (Rif), Rabbi Asher ben Yehiel (Rosh), Rabbi Mordechai ben Hillel (the *Mordechai*), and Rabbi Yosef Caro (the *Shulhan Arukh*).[8]

Parenthetically, in its version of the ruling, the Talmud Yerushalmi relates an incident involving Rabbi Yohanan, a talmudic sage of the third century. Apparently, in the course of his travels, the rabbi was introduced to an emaciated individual in dire need of a meal. Upon inquiring, Rabbi Yohanan learned that the man was the town schoolteacher, who as a sign of his religious devotion was given to fasting regularly. For this the rabbi reprimanded him severely.

Such behavior was unacceptable, he said, even among those pursuing more mundane occupations. Extreme religious devotion of this sort was an obstacle to the full energy and concentration that any worker owes to his employer. Surely one involved in nothing less than God's work, educating children in the ways of religious law and practice, can ill-afford misguided piety. The point resonates with the special responsibilities that belong to teachers alone. At the same time, it reinforces our understanding of the talmudic attitude toward worker productivity at large.

In closing his discussion related to the hire of workers and the lease of real estate and chattels, Maimonides cites the Tosefta almost verbatim.[9] Then, by way of summarizing the general attitude toward worker productivity, he adds: "Just as the employer is warned neither to steal the wages of the poor nor to oppress him, so too is the employee forewarned not to steal the labor of his employer by wasting a bit here and there and completing the day with trickery. Instead, he must be most demanding upon himself and his time."

Maimonides invokes the example of the biblical patriarch Jacob, who worked with all his energies for his father-in-law, Laban, and was rewarded handily by God, despite the treachery of his erstwhile employer, the father of his wife. If working so diligently was required despite the poor treatment and abuse that he suffered as an employee, surely it stands as a model for labor relations generally. Rabbi Vidal of Tolosa, in his commentary to the code of Maimonides, deviates from his usual practice of providing proof-text, citation, and precedent. Instead, he simply states that the point is self-evident.

Nevertheless, the ruling has its exemptions. Most obviously, in the case of independent contractors, an agreement can be made between the parties in advance that would include privileges of multiple employment.[10] Additionally, as we have noted, *minhag*, local custom and prevailing practice, also plays an important role in employee relations, as in many other contexts of Jewish life. Defined by geographic setting and/or industry standard, *minhag* is often invoked to help specify, modify, and even nullify the strict interpretation of the law.

Thus, as we have noted elsewhere, employment standards mandated by a strict reading of halakhah might require a worker to leave his home with the rising sun and remain at work until dark, following a series of talmudic inferences based on the works of the psalmist. However, this demand is nullified by local usage. Of course, a contrary stipulation may be stated in the employment contract, to which all parties must agree. Absent such stipulation, however, the employer is without prerogative in his attempt to demand a change in the customary workday, even if he offers to pay for the overtime (Bava Metzia 83b). The major rabbinic authorities, including Maimonides, Rabbi Yosef Caro, and Rabbi Moshe Isserles (Rema), cite this mishnah as binding, with no dissent.[11]

In some ways, this is less a matter of the preeminence of local usage than may superficially appear. Instead, it reflects a theme raised earlier: the discretion extended to the parties to a contract to tailor their agreement as they see fit. In this context, *minhag* is invoked as an implicit element in any employment contract. In a locality where such practices are well-known aspects of personnel management and employee relations, they can be taken as given. The absence of any stipulations at the time of the contract suggests that the prevailing business practice, in our case the standard workday, was acceptable to all parties to the agreement. An employer's subsequent attempt to demand a more rigorous work schedule becomes an abrogation of the spirit and the presumptions of the contract.

This is reflected in an early ruling by Rabbi Gershom Me'or ha-Golah. Regarding a teacher employed by the municipality, who had accepted tutoring and writing assignments after hours, he found that, absent prior arrangements to the contrary, "If it is customary for other teachers to be busy with their own affairs on their time, then this one may be busy as well, and no one may force upon him. . . . This Reuven, if he wrote a book at the time that other teachers are busy with their own needs, the permission is in his hands."[12]

As an aside, it is noteworthy that the subject of multiple employment among teachers, in particular, seems to have engendered a good deal of controversy. We have already discussed the concerns and admonitions of the talmudic sage Rabbi Yohanan. These seem to have been insufficient to prevent active moonlighting among teachers and equally sharp reactions among their employers, generally the *kehillah*, or local Jewish community, acting as a form of municipality in the public domain.

For example, in the seventeenth century, the administration of the Jewish elementary schools of Verona, the local authority for primary Jewish education in the community, found it necessary to remove any doubts about the contractual obligations of those under its employ. In its charter, dated 1688, the administration took great pains to enumerate several provisions banning teachers from accepting any other form of employment or study, "permanent or temporary, so that they will spend all their time studiously, in the study hall." Teachers were further proscribed from accepting new students without the express written permission of the administration.

Similar limitations and restrictions on the schedules of teachers are found in the charters of the Jewish communities of Cracow, Worms, Nikolsburg, Hamburg, Altona, and Grunwald during the same period. Apparently, such conflicts were common in Jewish communities of very different traditions, histories, and host cultures throughout Europe.[13] Perhaps they were engendered by more than just a concern about the sacred mission entrusted to the teaching profession.

It may be, as well, that teachers were more tempted to indulge in multiple employment because they had longer after-hours periods available to them than workers in other trades. Further, their compensation was rarely sufficient to

feed their families, an irony considering the storied commitment of the Jewish community, the "people of the book," to the
education of its young. Finally, their extra efforts largely
required an investment of time with little capital risk involved.
This may help to explain the high incidence of moonlighting
among contemporary educational practitioners in the United
States, noted above.

III

More recent sources offer other exemptions from the early
restrictions upon moonlighting. For an example, Rabbi Yehiel
Michael Epstein distinguishes between two types of employees: the full-time day-worker, known as a *po'el,* and the independent contractor or consultant, known as a *kablan.* The *po'el*
is generally a regular worker whose involvement after-hours is
of legitimate concern to his employer. Strenuous activity will
inevitably sap his physical strength and motivation during
normal business hours and prevent him from applying himself
fully. Consequently, he is proscribed from additional employment unless such an arrangement has been included in the
employment contract or approved by his employer.

By contrast, the *kablan* owes only a project-based commitment to his client and may pace himself as he sees fit. While he
is working on a particular job at a given time, his after-hours
activities are not subject to his employer's pleasure. He may
accept additional assignments at his own discretion. Indeed,
even if he accepts a commitment for a long-term project, the
kablan presumably would retain this prerogative, unless he
barters it away in the initial work agreement.[14]

Following this reasoning, contemporary writers have
extended the exemption in directions uncharted by precedent,

rendering the original thrust of the halakhah virtually nullified. For example, in his analysis of labor law in Jewish tradition, Wahrhaftig suggests that the proscriptions against multiple employment are time-bound and consequently hold little
relation to current conditions of work and the workplace.[15]

The mandates against multiple employment were rooted in
concerns about the diminution of an employee's energy at his
second job, considerations that make perfect sense where the
workday begins at dawn and continues until dark, the modal
abstract cited above. However, in contemporary Western society the workday is typically limited to eight hours or less.
Under these circumstances, employees are physically able to
engage in supplementary activities without impinging upon
their primary responsibilities. Sufficient time is now available
in the course of the workday so that even regular, full-time
employees can presume discretion over their own schedules,
as long as their responsibilities are fulfilled and their workload
completed. In this sense, the modern *po'el* assumes characteristics akin to those of the *kablan* of old.

In addition, Wahrhaftig argues that the traditional opposition to supplementary employment is rooted in a period when
workers had no reason to presume discretion over their schedules. If they were hired to do a job, it was their sole commitment. However, the modern work schedule, limited as it is to
the eight-hour day or the forty-hour week, makes such discretion tantamount to a *minhag*. It becomes an integral part of prevailing business practice and an assumed stipulation to the
work agreement. Any employer who would remove that discretion must so stipulate at the time of contract.

Levine strikes a still more progressive note. Beginning with
the same assumptions, he argues that the concern about supplemental employment raised by the halakhah derive from a

fear that the employee's stamina will be dissipated. However, work performance is not purely a function of hours served. It should be subject, therefore, to empirical evaluations by management to measure any adverse effects that result. The key criterion is whether taking extra work reduces the employee's productivity below the performance level of co-workers in identical jobs.[16]

Therefore, one may presume discretion to engage in supplementary employment even when no widespread practice of accepting outside work can be identified in a given profession. The logic is simple. A worker is engaged to maintain a given level of productivity on the job. Unless the worker is receiving extra compensation for additional service, his employer may only expect that his performance will match the industry standard both in quality and in hours of service. As long as that is maintained, he has no claim on the worker's after-hours time.

Conversely, a worker may presume the right to multiple employment only so long as his performance at his primary job continues to meet the industry standard. The specific criteria for review of his performance may be established as part of the original contract. Absent such stipulation, they may be presumed as equivalent to the average co-worker of similar rank and salary in the organization.

IV

The direct discussions of this issue in talmudic and rabbinic literature are generally content to consider only its most obvious aspects—the depletion of energy and motivation from the level the employer would normally have a right to expect from his workforce. Because productivity may suffer, an employee "is not permitted to fulfill his own responsibilities by night so that he can hire himself by day." However, regarding a second element of proprietary concern—potential conflicts of interest, access to information and clientele, and the tendency to work at private business during the workday—halakhah is largely silent.

Intuitively, however, it would seem that the thrust of the tradition would oppose supplemental employment on these grounds as well, even with no evidence of adverse effects on worker performance. This may be inferred, for example, from the exhortations of Maimonides cited above. A worker who takes time for his own projects or who subtly solicits clients during the course of the workday presumably would be guilty of "steal[ing] the labor of his employer" and "completing the day with trickery."

In addition, consider yet another talmudic source dealing with a related matter: "One who places his fellow in a shop for half the profit, if [the latter] was a craftsman, then he should not be busy with his craft, for his eyes will not be on the shop when he is involved with his craft. However, if his partner [the owner] was with him, he is permitted" (Tosefta Bava Metzia 4:7).

The major authorities cite this ruling as binding, adding that if the craftsman disregards the prohibition and profitably engages in his own business while on duty in the shop, then he is required to share his earnings with the owner. However, if the owner was in the shop with him: (a) full responsibility for the private work did not rest solely upon his shoulders; (b) we may assume that the owner was aware of what he was doing; and (c) objections, if any, could have been raised at the time. Absent such objection, the owner cedes this privilege to his partner.[17]

Yet no inferences are made here regarding employee relations. Rather, the terms "his fellow" and "half the profit" and the entire closing section are taken to suggest that this was a matter of partnership rather than employment or agency. Indeed, Maimonides includes this discussion in the laws of partnership. Rabbi Yosef Caro lists it among the laws of loans and interest, suggesting that one who uses a place of joint business for his own pursuits must share the profits with his partner, lest he be guilty of usury. Nevertheless, the application of this ruling to employees using the workday for their own purposes may be inferred.

Although he does not use the foregoing passage from the Tosefta as a proof-text, Rabbi Gershom Me'or ha-Golah appears to follow this precise line of reasoning. In his ruling about teachers accepting private work assignments after hours, cited above, it appears that the teacher in question also busied himself with his own private concerns during the school day. In this regard, Rabbi Gershom states:

> That he wrote during the hours when children are taught, if other teachers of that locale regularly do the same, then he is permitted. If not, then he may not. And if the employer was in the same locale and knew [of this conflict], then [the teacher] may be dismissed. . . . But since he was not dismissed, certainly [the employer] accepted and conceded and was satisfied.[18]

Though somewhat cryptic, his comments parallel the Tosefta, at least in part. Absent local custom to the contrary, using the regular workday for supplemental activities may be grounds for summary dismissal unless the employer knew of his worker's practice and issued no objections. This is tantamount to his "partner" sitting in the shop with him. The careful employer would be well advised to delineate such rules at the point of contract.

V

Several comments are in order by way of summary conclusion. First, it is obvious that the issue of multiple employment is neither new nor unique to current economic systems. Apparently it was a well-known practice even in the ancient world, and enough of a concern to require regulation by the time of the Tosefta, no later than the second century of the common era. In fact, the character of the regulation was somewhat unique. Notwithstanding the general inclination in support of labor and workers' rights that typifies classical Jewish writings, here normative statements regarding moonlighting appear to favor the employer. This, of course, presumes the absence of a *minhag*, a customary and prevailing business practice that tends otherwise.

In applying the tradition, therefore, it becomes crucial to determine how the existence of a *minhag* is identified and established legally. The most obvious is that it simply emerges historically; in other words, that it is based on prior practice, long-standing usage, and public acceptance. As such it is a microcosm of Jewish social and communal traditions over time, rooted in the informal understandings that underpin and reinforce social relations and provide their stability and cement. Only later are they given formal sanction in legal or ecclesiastical decision, frequently in response to a test emerging from some dispute in their application due to their informal structure. The phenomenon is well known in Jewish tradition and employed even in the face of logic and legislation to the contrary.

With current technological advances, it may also be possible to establish *minhag* quantitatively, that is, based on formal count. This would mean surveying an area or its businesses and determining what attitudes or presuppositions prevail among those engaged in a given trade or industry. To do so would have a subtle impact on the *minhag* as a legal category usually taken to be fairly static, with change coming slowly and only with great deliberation. It also would guard against the tendency for *minhag* to become self-fulfilling; that is, because it is given quasi-legal credibility, it becomes customary business practice, rather than the other way around.

As a matter of application, a survey of business practices would require periodic review to test whether presuppositions and practices have changed over time. This would release a creative dynamism in the usage of *minhag* and move it closer to a different category of reasoning employed in Jewish thought. To evidence an assertion of a prevailing attitude or behavior, the rabbis often invoke the concept known as *rov* in Hebrew and as *rubah* in Aramaic. This refers to a numerical majority identified by assumptive or anecdotal reasoning (*de lessah kamon*) or by empirical evidence (*de eeyssah kamon*).

Whichever method we choose to help establish the *minhag*, it will also be necessary to define its parameters. For an example, we might opt for geographic parameters, asking us to determine the prevailing business practice of a given locale or community, a method that must accommodate the newcomer as well as the highly mobile and often geographically disjointed history of the Jewish people. Alternatively, we might look at standards in the relevant industry or profession, local usage notwithstanding. Here workers in different trades would be treated differentially even if they lived and worked in the same locale.

The issue is sharpened when we glance anew at the United States government statistics cited at the beginning of this chapter. The fact that more than seven million workers are engaged in multiple employment appears to suggest the emergence of a commonplace in the American economy. Yet they constitute a mere 6.2 percent of the national workforce. Is this a sufficient proportion by which to establish a *minhag*? That the proportions are higher among, say, managerial employees, police officers, and university instructors turns the argument about once more. Furthermore, independent studies suggest that official government figures are likely to yield a substantial undercount, since respondents often have a strong motivation not to be candid with representatives of federal agencies empowered to collect such data.[19]

Finally, the Tosefta passage on which the position to multiple employment was based was concerned that, by working after hours, an employee "will sap his strength, weaken his mind, and not do his work energetically." Presumably, those who ruled in its favor follow the same line of reasoning. However, empirical study indicates that this fear may be exaggerated. Though far from conclusive, research assessing the capacities of moonlighters has found no significant differences between them and other employees.

In studying job stress, emotional and physical health, job performance, motivation, and absenteeism, researchers find that moonlighters appear no worse off, no more likely to underperform or to behave in an undesirable fashion. Indeed, ironic as it may seem, some data suggest that they exhibit higher levels of job satisfaction and are more likely to be socially active than those who do not moonlight.[20] These and future findings must be filtered into decisions regarding existence of a *minhag* or the application of earlier rulings in evaluating current aspects of employee relations and worker rights.

1. John F. Stinson, "New Data on Multiple Jobholding Available from the CPS," *Monthly Labor Review* 120 (1997): 3–8; Michael Hopkins and Jeffrey L. Seglin, "Americans@work," *Inc* 19 (1997): 77–85; "Multiple Jobholders by Selected Demographic and Economic Characteristics," *Employment and Earnings* 6 (1999): 67; "Moonlighting for Moola," *American Demographics* 19 (1997): 41; Bill Leonard, "Rate of Moonlighting Among Workers Holds a Steady Pace," *Human Resources Magazine* 42, no. 7 (1997): 10; Jean Kimmel and Lisa M. Powell, "Moonlighting Trends and Related Policy Issues in Canada and the United States," *Canadian Public Policy* 25 (1999): 207–231; More Europeans Are Moonlighting," *Futurist* 31 (May–June 1997): 14; "Moonlighting on the Rise," *Worklife Report* 10 (1997): 18; Diane Crispell, "Multiple Jobholding Reached Record High in May 1989," *Bureau of Labor Statistics News* 89-529 (1989): 1–5.

2. W. David Allen, "The Moonlighting Decisions of Unmarried Men and Women: Family and Labor Market Influences," *Atlantic Economic Journal* 26 (1998): 190–205; Margaret K. Nelson, "Between Paid and Unpaid Work: Gender Patterns in Supplemental Economic Activities Among White, Rural Families," *Gender and Society* 13, no. 4 (1999): 518–539; Donna Dempster and Phyllis Moen, "Moonlighting Husbands: A Life-Cycle Perspective," *Work and Occupations* 16 (February 1989): 43-64; John Stinson "Moonlighting by Women Jumped to Record Highs," *Monthly Labor Review* 109 (November 1986): 22–25.

3. John Stinson, "Multiple Jobholding Up Sharply in the 1980's," *Monthly Labor Review* 113 (1990): 3–10.

4. An analysis of the full literature regarding multiple employment is beyond our objectives. A cross-disciplinary review would include C. Little, "Sociological Moonlighting: Practical Advice About Consulting for Local Government," *Sociological Practice Review* 2 (1991): 217–223; M. H. Taylor and A. E. Filmer, "Moonlighting: The Practical Problems," *Canadian Public Administration* 29 (1986): 592–597; Steven Culler and Gloria Bazzoli, "The Moonlighting Decisions of Resident Physicians," *Journal of Health Economics* 4 (1985): 283–292; Cathy May, "Moonlighting: It's a Question of DP Ethics," *Data Management* 23 (1985): 10; Robert Wisniewski and Paul Kliene, "Teacher Moonlighting: An Unstudied Phenomenon," *Phi*

Delta Kappan 65 (1984): 553–555; R. M. Pipkin (1982), "Moonlighting in Law School," *American Bar Association Research Journal,* 1982, pp. 1109–1162; Carlton J. Snow and Elliott M. Abramson, "By the Light of Dual Employment: Standards for Employer Regulation of Moonlighting," *Indiana Law Journal* 55 (1979–80): 581–614.

5. R. Factor, "Moonlighting: Why Training Programs Should Monitor Residents' Activities," *Hospital and Community Psychiatry* 42 (1991): 738; Jeffrey Raffel and Lance Groff, "Shedding Light on the Dark Side of Teacher Moonlighting," *Educational Evaluation and Policy Analysis* 12 (1990): 403–414; Edward Pawlak and June Bays, "Executive Perspectives on Part-Time Private Practice," *Administration in Social Work* 12 (1988): 1–11; Jeffrey Davidson, "Curtail Moonlighting with Solid Guidelines and Performance Evaluations," *Data Management* 24 (1986): 26–27; John Keely and James Ryan, "Should Police Moonlight in Security Jobs?" *Security Management* 27 (1983): 9–18.

6. See John Stinson, "Moonlighting: A Key to Differences in Employment Growth," *Monthly Labor Review* 110 (1987): 30–31; Richard Upton, "Moonlighting: A Dark Shadow on the White Economy," *Personnel Management* 12 (1980): 28–31.

7. Alice LaPlante, "Outside Work OK if You Ask," *Computerworld* 25 (1991): 101; Ronald Factor, "What Residents Do in Their Free Time Is Their Decision," *Hospital and Community Psychiatry* 42 (1991): 739–42; James Whitley, "Moonlighting: A Good Educational Experience for Residents," *Investigative Radiology* 22 (1987): 693; Alan Arcuri et al., "Moonlighting by Police Officers: A Way of Life," *Psychological Reports* 60 (1987): 210–211; Sole Santangelo and David Lester, "Correlates of Job Satisfaction of Public School Teachers: Moonlighting, Locus of Control and Stress," *Psychological Reports* 58 (1985): 130; Bruce W. Fraser, "The Moonlight Shines on White Collars," *Nation's Business* 71 (1983): 52–53; Bill Waddell, "Authorized Moonlighting," *Business Forum,* Spring 1983, p. 32.

8. Rabbi Yitzhak Alfasi, Bava Metzia 52b; Rabbi Asher ben Yehiel, Bava Metzia 7:3; Rabbi Mordekhai ben Hillel, Bava Metzia 343; Rabbi Yosef Caro, *Shulhan Arukh,* Hoshen Mishpat 337:19.

9. Rabbi Moshe Maimonides, *Yad ha-Hazakah,* Hilkhot Sekhirut 13:7

10. See, e.g., Tosafot Bava Metzia 83a, s.v. *ha-sokher*.

11. See Rabbi Moshe Maimonides, *Yad*, Hilkhot Sekhirut 9:1; Rabbi Yosef Caro, *Shulhan Arukh*, Hoshen Mishpat 331:1, and the comments of the Rema ad loc.

12. Shelomoh Eidelberg, *Teshuvot Rabbenu Gershom Me'or ha-Golah* (New York, 1955), no. 92, pp. 167–168.

13. See Shillem Wahrhaftig, *Dinei Avodah be-Mishpat ha-Ivri* (Jerusalem, 1969), pp. 490–492.

14. Rabbi Yehiel Michael Epstein, *Arukh ha-Shulhan*, Hoshen Mishpat 337:28. Distinctions between the *po`el* and the *kablan* are well known in the halakhic literature, relating, for example, to the rights of the latter to set his own time schedule, or of the former to rescind a commitment unilaterally with almost no prejudice. However, regarding multiple employment, the point appears unique to this analysis. For a summary of the differences between the two categories, see, e.g., Rabbi Yaakov ben Asher, *Tur Shulhan Arukh*, Hoshen Mishpat 333:2.

15. Warhaftig, *Dinei Avodah be Mishpat ha-Ivri*, pp. 330–334.

16. Aaron Levine, *Economics and Jewish Law* (New York:Ktav, 1987), pp. 180–181.

17. See Rabbi Moshe Maimonides, *Yad*, Hilkhot Sheluhim ve-Shutafin 7:7; Rabbi Yosef Caro, *Shulhan Arukh*, Yoreh De`ah 177:29

18. See Eidelberg, *Teshuvot Rabbenu Gershom Me'or ha-Golah*, p. 168.

19. See Vishwanath Baba and Muhammad Jamal, "How Much Do We Really Know About Moonlighters?" *Public Personnel Management* 21 (1992): 65–73; Dempster and Moen, "Moonlighting Husbands."

20. Baba and Jamal, "How Much Do We Really Know About Moonlighters?" Also Muhammad Jamal, "Is Moonlighting Mired in Myth?" *Personnel Journal* 67 (1988): 48–53; idem, "Moonlighting: Personal, Social and Organizational Consequences," *Human Relations* 39 (1986): 977–990; idem and Ronald Crawford, "Consequences of Extended Work Hours: A Comparison of Moonlighters, Overtimers and Modal Employees," *Human Resources Management* 20 (1981): 18–23.

7

Look for the Union Label
Organized Labor and Collective Bargaining

I

Jews have been actively involved in the American labor movement since its inception, particularly in the "lighter" industries and needle trades of the urban northeast. Beginning late in the nineteenth century, the immigrant Jewish community produced both an active workers' press and an array of labor luminaries, including Samuel Gompers, Abraham Cahan, Daniel De Leon, and Joseph Barondess. They founded the International Ladies Garment Workers' Union, the United Hebrew Trades, the Cloakmakers' Union, and the Workmen's Circle, and were involved in a wide variety of activities on behalf of workers' rights and socialist initiatives.[1]

Moreover, the Jewish commitment to labor in the modern era was not limited to the United States. Around the same time that Samuel Gompers was helping to organize the AFL and Daniel De Leon was attempting to bring the Knights of Labor under his socialist leadership, Jewish immigrants to Palestine

An earlier version of this paper appeared as "Ba-aley Umanut: Organized Labor and the Jewish Tradition" in Yaakov Ellman and Jeffrey Gurock (eds.), *Hazon Nahum: Studies in Jewish Law, History and Thought Presented to Dr. Norman Lamm on His 70th Birthday* (New York: Ktav, 1997).

were establishing agricultural settlements under the banner and ideology of labor or socialist Zionism. From the late nineteenth century through the end of World War II, a broad spectrum of social and political institutions were created there, under the leadership of newly arrived European Jews and their children, all in advance of the establishment of the State of Israel.

Included were numerous agricultural collectives known as kibbutzim and moshavim, along with a broad-based centralized trade union, the Histadrut, that served as an umbrella organization for most areas of the economy. These were undergirded by several political parties whose ideologies varied from left-leaning laborist thought to outright Marxism. Reflected in the thinking of Nahman Syrkin, A. D. Gordon, and Berl Katzenelson and in the political leadership of David Ben-Gurion, Moshe Sharett, and Golda Meir, labor socialism was a singular force in the emergence of political Zionism and the founding of the State of Israel.[2]

Expressions of labor ideology also were evident among those Jews who remained in Eastern Europe. Their major organizational manifestation was the Jewish Workers' League, known as the Bund. Though short-lived by comparison to its counterparts in the United States or Palestine, the Bund was organized during a stormy period of confrontation and violence. Formed in 1897 around a group of intellectuals and theorists known as the Vilna Circle, it provided focus for Jewish support of Russian democratic socialism at the turn of the century. Behind the efforts of Arkady Kremer, Aaron Lieberman, and Vladimir Kosovsky, it left its mark on early attempts at socialist reform before the Russian Revolution of 1917. In that way, it also eased the passage of Jews into mainstream communist leadership with the rise of the Soviet Union.[3]

Hebrew Scripture was often invoked as a rallying call for these cross-national Jewish commitments to the cause of labor and the working class. The Bible propounds the principle of inherent human equality before God, seeing the faithful as servants of the Lord rather than as servants of His servants (Leviticus 25:55). Consequently, as explained in an earlier chapter, hired workers were permitted to eat of their employer's produce while on the job (Deuteronomy 23:25–26) and were to receive their wages within the day (Leviticus 19:13, Deuteronomy 24:14–15). Servants indentured as restitution for a crime or by virtue of debt likewise were to be treated with kindness and respect (Leviticus 25:39–53). Upon the completion of their indenture, generally no more than six years, they were to be liberally rewarded "out of thy flock and out of thy threshing floor and out of thy winepress" (Deuteronomy 15:12–14).

Building on these inspiring passages, Jewish authorities, over a period of some twenty centuries, were often called upon to adjudicate disputes between workers and management, applying biblical principle to everyday practice. They considered the impact of labor relations on the local economy and evaluated claims of protectionism against foreign workers. They further involved themselves in various forms of economic regulation in disparate historical and geographic contexts, from pagan Rome, Christian Europe, and the Muslim empire to the contemporary West. Talmudic sages, medieval rabbinic thinkers, and modern interpreters of the tradition all found expression in Jewish sources, generally supporting the creation and the operation of collective labor organization long before its advent and legitimacy in Europe or the United States.

This chapter will survey attitudes toward organized labor and trade unions as reflected in classical Jewish texts and sources. Particular emphasis will focus upon the development of early labor cooperatives under Jewish authority, and the discretion extended them to set internal standards and sanctions, bar the use of non-union labor, and declare strikes and job actions. The closing section will consider the implications of these findings for the contemporary organization and regulation of unions and collective bargaining units.

II

The principle that members of a trade or craft may set standards to regulate the conditions of employment, and that they may enforce these standards, has a long and well-established history in Jewish tradition. True to its general predisposition, these rulings have generally favored workers, though not without important limitations in the face of overriding public interest. Recent aspects of labor relations, such as work stoppages, sanctions against strikebreaking, and the closed shop, have been more controversial.

The right to collective action derives from the basic powers extended to the board or council of any community. The Talmud (Bava Batra 8b) records that "the townsfolk may set weights and measures, fix the wages of workers, and apply sanctions against infractions." Labor collectives, by industry or by trade, were seen as a subset of communal administration, with similar powers provided by analogy.

The Tosefta (Bava Metzia 11:12), a variant collection of early talmudic rulings, offers the following illustrations:

> Textile workers and dyers may decide that all material brought into town will be processed collectively. Bakers may

establish their work shifts, and donkey drivers may say, "To whomsoever [among us] a donkey dies, we will replace it for him." If it dies through negligence, they are not required to replace it. . . . Merchant seamen may say, "To whomsoever [among us] a ship is lost, we will replace it for him.". . . And if he went to a place where no one goes [and it was lost], they need not replace it for him.

These first examples of trade or labor collectives were empowered to apportion work and set hours. They also organized cooperative programs of insurance and security against loss, especially in trades where such eventualities were common, such as transport and shipping. As with civil administration, these groups could "apply sanctions against infractions," for they had internal powers of adjudication and enforcement by which they could require collective coverage for loss and review claims against negligence or undue risk.

Their discretion was subject to regulation, however. Thus, the same talmudic discussion (Bava Batra 8b) records the following in regard to an ancient labor dispute over internal discipline and the right to sanction: "Butchers arranged among themselves that if one should work on the day assigned to his fellow, a skin [of his animal] shall be destroyed. One worked on the day of his fellow and they destroyed the skin. They appeared before Rava, who required that they make restitution."

The rabbis objected to Rava's decision, citing the earlier ruling that "townsfolk" may enforce their regulations, a reference that includes members of a trade as well. Said Rabbi Papa: "This is true if there is no important person in the town, but if there is an important person, it makes no difference that they have made regulations." To be valid and enforceable among all members of a local trade or profession, the conditions set by labor leaders apparently had to be stipulated before the "important person in the town." In this case, Rava, a third-century talmudic figure, was empowered to adjudicate civil matters. Without his assent, arrangements made by a group of butchers, or any other labor collective, were null and void. Attempts to enforce them would be actionable and subject to redress.

Over the following centuries, these powers and their limits were detailed and codified through case law and systematic review. For example, the talmudic precedent restricted itself to a consideration of the rights of independent contractors, such as butchers and merchant seaman, as members of something akin to a guild. By and large, medieval Jewish authorities hesitated to differentiate between employees by the nature of their contractual obligations in this respect. Consequently, day workers and full-time laborers were assigned the same rights to organize and to set internal standards as self-employed contractors and yeomen.

By the same token, validation by an "important person" was understood to mean a sage versed in law and custom, empowered to "correct the actions of the state and bring success to the path of its residents." Regulation was subject less to religious authority than to the powers of one appointed as a municipal executive or administrator.[4]

Authorities differed, however, as to the reach of this veto. Some suggested that any labor stipulation required executive confirmation, if only from respect and honor for communal authority.[5] Most held, however, that workers were generally free to set internal standards without interference. Validation was only necessary for regulations bearing on the public interest. This was loosely defined to include innovations to generally accepted business practice that might have a direct financial impact upon the consumer.[6]

In the talmudic case discussed above, for example, the butchers required validation by the executive because allotting one tradesman per day had economic ramifications far beyond merely establishing more equitable work shifts. It effectively reduced competition, keeping the cost of labor artificially high and increasing the price of meat as a result. Instances that were more clearly related to internal administration, as in the collective insurance arrangements noted earlier, required no such executive validation.[7]

Given the provenance of their powers, labor collectives soon became embroiled in complex debates over the breadth of the public mandate and over civil governance in Jewish tradition, debates that presaged or paralleled the emergence of secular democratic theory elsewhere in Europe. Scholars differed, for example, over the amount of member support necessary before public decisions could bear authority and sanction. Some demanded full or near unanimity, as they did in the debate over civil authority generally, lest the minority remain unprotected.[8]

Others argued that the analogy between a political community and a labor collective was faulty. Perhaps a majority might suffice in communal decisions, since all residents were, by their very presence, members of the civitas. Their mere attendance evidenced their interests. However, among members of a trade, it first was necessary to establish such a community. Consequently, some demanded unanimity for all decisions involved in founding the collective, and some, still more stringent, were satisfied with nothing less than unanimous support for subsequent decisions as well.[9]

Still, mainstream, authoritative opinion argued that a majority would suffice. It did insist, however, that at the very least, all members of the trade retain the right to participate in

the relevant deliberations.[10] In more recent times, most authorities have adapted the same position, based on legal reasoning
as much as on local practice sanctioned by secular authority.
As a result, Jewish tradition now generally considers a union's
regulations, if supported by a majority, to be binding upon all
its members.[11]

III

While the early sources offer precious little about the legitimacy
of decisions to strike, the Talmud does provide some detail about
what appears to be the ancient equivalent of a collective job
action by some of the Temple priests (Yoma 38a, Shekalim 14a,
Tosefta Yoma 2:5, Yerushalmi Yoma 3:9). Evidently, both the
House of Garmu, bakers of the sacred "shewbread," and the
House of Avtinas, charged with sifting the sacred incense,
refused to train others in their delicate crafts. In this manner they
maintained an effective monopoly on their special products and
services. In response the sages summoned more amenable arti-
sans from Alexandria to train novice priests in these arts and
thereby broaden the available labor pool, as it were.

They soon found the skills of these early "strike-breakers"
inadequate, however. As a result, they were forced to double
the wages of Garmu and Avtinas before they would return to
work. While the leaders of each house maintained that they
were not motivated by a purely pecuniary attempt to establish
hegemony over their craft, the talmudic commentaries suggest
that they were not believed.[12] Nevertheless, the priests
returned to their posts and enjoyed their newfound affluence
with impunity.

The case raises several interesting points. We have just
noted that decisions made by employee groups are subject to

executive confirmation, especially when they affect the public interest, as with Rava and his butchers. Why was their no such consideration here? To be sure, the Talmud is most explicit in its displeasure with the priests of Garmu and Avtinas. Still, there is no record of an attempt to invalidate their actions. In fact their demands were accepted in full, despite considerable cost to the public coffers.

While the commentaries are silent on this issue, two speculations are in order. First, Garmu and Avtinas may have been less an example of a strike than of a "lockout." It was the sages who replaced these priests, in retaliation for their intransigence, a decision that proved a bit rash. It was left for them, therefore, to convince Garmu and Avtinas to return. This they did by negotiating what was, in effect, a new contract.

Alternatively, requirements that labor actions be stipulated before the "important person in the town" may have been rooted as a precedent at the court of Rava, and not before. This would date such developments to about the fourth century C.E. in the Jewish community of Babylonia, some two hundred years after the Temple was destroyed by the legions of Rome. Consequently, the sages who confronted these priestly demands had no such administrative tool at their command and therefore were forced to acquiesce. Ironically, none of the classic commentaries raises these issues. The case of Avtinas and Garmu passes virtually unnoticed among them as a precedent for labor relations.

It is revealing, however, that the incident occurred in the public sector. As we will demonstrate at length elsewhere, Jewish tradition holds those who toil for the public weal to unusually high standards of quality, productivity, and personal ethics.[13] They also have special claims to job security akin to modern tenure provisions.[14] Most important here, the priests of Avtinas and Garmu suffered no special limits upon their right to strike, their public commission notwithstanding.

By and large, these concerns are largely ignored by medieval Jewish thinkers, suggesting the absence of any persistent or systematic pressure in that direction. This changed with the modern emergence of large and assertive trade unions and the various political movements that arose in their support, especially toward the end of the nineteenth century. Given the importance of labor ideology in the foundation of the Zionist movement and the early history of Israel, contemporary Jewish authorities have sought to attend these issues in light of the tradition. Within specified limits, most have confirmed the early talmudic dicta.

Generally, present-day authorities have found in favor of the rights of employees to strike, to impose discipline among members, to prevent strike-breaking, and to keep employers from using non-union labor. Within these broad junctures, however, opinion diverges. For example, Rabbi Ben-Zion Ouziel, an early Chief Rabbi of Israel's Sephardic communities, found no inherent right for workers to take unilateral action. Strikes cause damage and loss to all concerned, he reasoned. The appropriate course of action is to have both sides appear before a properly constituted court or other mutually acceptable system of binding arbitration, with no interruption of work and productivity.[15]

His Ashkenazic colleague, Rabbi Avraham Yitzhak Kook, agreed that any dispute between workers and management should be submitted to arbitration. For him, this was a simple corollary to judicial or executive approval for labor decisions that have an impact upon the public interest. If management refuses to appear, however, or fails to abide by the arbitrator's ruling, then a union is within its rights to call a strike or take some other unilateral job action.[16]

Rabbi Eliezer Waldenberg, a contemporary scholar in Jerusalem, assumes an even more liberal position.[17] Unilateral action without court approval has a long-standing place in Jewish legal tradition, he argues. Based upon the talmudic dictum that "one may act upon the law on his own" (Bava Kamma 27b), he cites Maimonides, who records: "A person may execute judgment for himself if the power is in his hands. When he acts by the faith and the law, he need not be troubled to go to court, even if there would have been no financial loss had he tarried and come to court."[18]

Later authorities emphasize the phrase "if the power is in his hands." They saw it as implying the right to employ necessary force in executing unilateral judgment. Applied to the realm of collective bargaining, this precedent is understood to suggest that if management has violated a contractual agreement, a legal obligation, or a long-standing employment practice, labor may take unilateral action. Under these circumstances, workers could call a general strike without first resorting to arbitration.[19]

Following a related line of reasoning, Rabbi Waldenberg disallows strike-breaking or the use of non-union labor. He reaches toward a related talmudic injunction against "entering into the livelihood" of another (Bava Batra 21b). Thus,

> if a resident of a court was a tradesman or had a shop or a mill, and a second came to enter his trade or to open a shop or a mill, [the former] may prevent him, assuming [the latter] is from another town. . . . So too residents of one town may prevent those of another, who do not pay tax with them, from bringing goods for sale or entering to broker loans.[20]

Support is drawn from an earlier ruling reminiscent of unilateral initiative. It holds that town residents, feeling fiscally endangered by interlopers but unable to make their case before the Jewish courts, may respond radically. They may "shut the gate in their [competitor's] face, whether through the local noble or through any preventive; it is simple that the right is in their hands, and only a fool would disagree." Under strictly limited circumstances, therefore, social concerns may justify circumvention of Jewish communal jurisdiction and permit redress before the secular authorities.[21]

Based on the analogy between residents of a town and members of a labor collective, this precedent is made to speak to strike-breaking activity. Non-union labor may be kept from participating in the local labor market because they stem, metaphorically, from "another town," that is, from outside the union. When a labor dispute occurs, strike-breakers are doubtless "entering into the livelihood" of their striking colleagues and therefore can be enjoined from such action by any available means.[22]

The right of locals to bar foreign competition is not universally accepted, however. The dissenters argue that the injunction against outsiders plying their trades freely in towns other than their own presumes no consequence to the consumer. They may be kept out to protect local commerce only if their prices and services are little different from what is already available. However, this is not the case where protecting local business artificially inflates prices. In this case, "logic dictates that to enact a ruling on behalf of merchants that will cause loss to consumers, this right they do not have."[23]

Unlike the other authorities, however, Rabbi Moshe Feinstein invoked prevailing business practice, secular legislation, and the economic climate as primary sources for pro-labor rulings. Though innovative, he was merely following the general tendency to give precedence to local custom in economic and social concerns. Thus Rabbi Feinstein argued that a strike is permissible regardless of the point in contention or the circumstances of negotiations. Rather, the logic inheres in the absence of an "important person" to regulate labor relations. Since no such executive has been empowered, and since American labor law has given legitimacy to job-stoppage as a labor strategy, decisions made by unions are legal and binding upon all their members.[24]

Recent rulings have supported bans on strike-breaking even when it may be harmful to consumers. This follows the claim that, traditional Jewish sources notwithstanding, collective job actions have been confirmed by secular legislation and by executive or judicial authority. As such, union initiative has entered the realm of customary business practice. Since this is the status of labor relations in Western societies today, these actions fit the contours of Jewish tradition and are fully enforceable and sanctioned. Aside from juridical considerations, strike-breaking is banned for practical reasons. In Rabbi Feinstein's words: "It has already been agreed by all residents of this country that it is a terrible violation to be hired in [the striker's] place." Nevertheless, while unions may take action to protect and improve the working conditions of their members, they may not condone violence, whether against management or dissenting workers.[25]

Finally, a unique public interest is recognized in certain services, and this requires that practitioners be more stringently regulated. A work stoppage by teachers in religious schools, for example, would constitute an intolerable interruption of instruction and a "violation of the tradition." Hospital and related health-care services and the provision of power and energy are also singled out as services whose cessation would create a public emergency. Employees in these areas are never permitted to strike, and their disputes must be submitted to binding arbitration immediately.[26]

IV

This survey of Jewish attitudes toward labor organization and collective job action yields several interesting contrasts with the history of the labor movement in the United States. The most obvious is that the former emerges from a millennial tradition of acceptance, while the latter was born in strife and violence. The American labor movement carries a legacy of militant confrontation over basic principles, such as the right to organize, to engage in collective bargaining with management, and to use collective job action in support of its cause. From the Haymarket riot to the Homestead lockout to the Pullman strike, the industrial front-line was nothing less than a battleground. The hostility faced there was matched in the halls of Congress and in the courts, where legislation and injunction were used as weapons against burgeoning trade unions.[27]

The conflict was eventually resolved in favor of the worker through the Norris-La Guardia Act (1932) and the Wagner Act (1935), in the wake of the Great Depression and the New Deal. The private employee's right to collective bargaining was protected with basic machinery created to enforce these rights and to sanction against their violation. It was reinforced by minimum-wage legislation, bans on child labor, and the creation of federal jobs programs.

Nevertheless, a series of developments over the past decades have curtailed some of labor's victories and compromised its hard-won position. One such challenge is the growth of the public sector of the labor market. In its initial labor legislation, the programs of the New Deal era specifically excluded public employees from many of the rights obtained by those under private employment. It was not until 1978 that federal law extended parallel rights to civil service workers, while state employees were still remanded to the good faith of their respective legislatures.

Many states and municipalities have extended similar rights to their employees. Still, the continued growth of public employment as a proportion of the workforce has significant implications for the directions of the labor movement generally.[28] This is matched by waning support for classical unionism in the courts and Congress, and also among members of labor's own constituency. The Taft-Hartley Act and other post–World War II legislation restricted many of the gains won during the New Deal. From the seventies to the early nineties, union membership in the United States fell, stabilizing at about seventeen million members.[29]

By contrast, Jewish tradition and practice has suffered no such ruptures. From its scriptural base, it harbored strong pro-labor sentiments. The position was expanded and expounded by those who were the arbiters and interpreters of the tradition through legislation and homily. The results were early models of labor organization and regulation. Indeed, the examples of collective labor action in talmudic writ appear to allow considerable discretion to labor organization, even in the face of official objections.

In the minds of the rabbis, labor organization was so obvious an element of the social environment that it derived from and analogized to municipal authority. As the residents of a town form a natural community of interests to be unified and directed under the auspices of representative leadership, so too the members of a trade. As the former protect their prerogatives through regulation and sanction, so too must the latter have similar discretion. Despite individual points of contention and the need for periodic adjudication, there is little dissent on principle.

The ascent of large public employee organizations provides no challenge to this commitment. Jewish tradition makes little distinction between the public and private sectors in apportioning the rights of employees to organize and to regulate their work standards. Public employees reap particular benefits in the form of job security and may be held to higher standards of quality and accountability due to their public trust. Yet, no special exclusions inhere in their status, and their right to strike is not limited. Indeed the most explicit account of a job action provided by the Talmud deals with Temple priests performing a public religious service.

However, Jewish thought is also marked by a sense of obligation to the corporate whole, an obligation that overrides individual rights or class interests. Even the elemental commitment to labor rights, therefore, is subject to the validation of executive and judicial authority. Especially when internal standards may impinge upon consumer interests, regulations set by a labor organization must be stipulated before a sage versed in statecraft and appointed as community leader. As a consequence, while the right to strike is not limited, and public employees share this freedom with their private-sector colleagues, all authorities agree that any job action that threatens the public interest must be remanded to binding arbitration. Essential services must not be suspended, whether provided by public authority or private initiative.

1. Hanita Blumfield, "Jewish Women Sew the Union Label," *Humanity and Society* 6, no. 1 (1982): 33–45; Morris Schappes, "The Political Origins of the Hebrew Trades," *Journal of Ethnic Studies* 5, no. 1 (1977): 13–44; Henry Feingold, *Zion In America* (New York: Hippocrene, 1974); see also Benjamin Wolkinson, "Labor and the

Jewish Tradition: A Reappraisal," *Jewish Social Studies* 40, nos. 3–4 (1977): 231–238.

2. Howard Sachar, *The Course of Modern Jewish History* (New York: Delta, 1976); Arthur Hertzberg, *The Zionist Idea: A Historical Analysis and Reader* (New York: Atheneum, 1975).

3. Nora Levin , *While Messiah Tarried: Jewish Socialist Movements, 1871–1917* (New York: Schocken, 1977); Salo Baron, *The Russian Jew Under Czars and Soviets* (New York: Macmillan, 1976).

4. Rabbi Moshe Maimonides, *Yad ha-Hazakah,* Hilkhot Mekhirah 14:11; see also Rabbi Asher ben Yehiel, *Hiddushei ha-Rosh,* Bava Batra 9a; Rabbi Menahem Me'iri, *Beit ha-Behirah,* Bava Batra 9a; Rabbi Yosef Caro, *Beit Yosef,* Hoshen Mishpat 231:30; Rabbi Yosef Caro, *Shulhan Arukh,* Hoshen Mishpat 231:28.

5. E.g., Rabbi Yom Tov Ishbili, *Hiddushei ha-Ritva,* Bava Batra 9a.

6. Rabbi Nissim Gerondi, *Hiddushei ha-Ran,* Bava Batra 9a; Rabbi Yosef Caro, *Beit Yosef,* Hoshen Mishpat 231:30; Rabbi Moshe Isserles, Hoshen Mishpat 231:30.

7. Rabbi Moshe Maimonides, *Yad ha Hazakeh,* Hilkhot Gezelah ve-Avedah 12:12, 15; Rabbi Yosef Caro, *Shulhan Arukh,* Hoshen Mishpat 272:16, 18.

8. E.g., Rabbi Yaakov Tam, cited in Rabbi Mordechai ben Hillel, *Mordekhai,* Bava Batra, 480–483.

9. Rabbi Yitzhak al-Barceloni, cited in Rabbi Vidal of Tolosa, *Maggid Mishneh,* Hilkhot Mekhirah 14:10; Rabbi Moshe ben Nahman, *Hiddushei ha-Ramban:* Bava Batra 9a; Rabbi Moshe Isserles, Hoshen Mishpat 231:28, Rabbi Yehiel Epstein, *Arukh ha-Shulhan,* Hoshen Mishpat 231:27.

10. Rabbi Yosef Caro, *Shulhan Arukh,* Hoshen Mishpat 231:28.

11. Rabbi Moshe Feinstein, *Iggerot Moshe:* Hoshen Mishpat 59; Rabbi Ovadiah Yosef, *She'elot u-Teshuvot Yehaveh Da'at* 4:48; Rabbi Eliezer Waldenberg, *Ziz Eliezer* 2:23.

12. Rabbi Shmuel Edels, *Hiddushei Aggadot ha-Maharsha,* Yoma 38a; Rabbi Ovadiah Bar-Tenora, *Perush ha-Ra'av,* Yoma 3:11; see also J. David Bleich, *Contemporary Halachic Problems* (New York: Yeshiva University Press, 1977).

13. E.g., Rabbi Moshe Maimonides, *Yad ha-Hazakah,* Hilkhot Sekhirut 10:7; Rabbi Yosef Caro, *Beit Yosef,* Hoshen Mishpat 306:12.

14. E.g., Rabbi Moshe Maimonides, *Yad,* Hilkhot Kelei ha-Mikdash 4:21; Rabbi Yom Tov Ishbili, *Hiddushei ha-Ritva,* Makkot 13a.

15. Rabbi Ben-Zion Ouziel, *Mishpatei Ouziel* 42:6.

16. Rabbi Abraham Kook, cited in Rabbi Kasriel Tkhursh, "Dinei Shevitot be-Halakhah," *Shanah be-Shanah,* 1963.

17. Rabbi Eliezer Waldenberg, *Ziz Eliezer* 2:23.

18. Rabbi Moshe Maimonides, *Yad,* Hilkhot Sanhedrin 2:12.

19. Rabbi Avraham di Biton, *Lehem Mishneh,* Hilkhot Sanhedrin 2:12; Rabbi Asher ben Yehiel, *Piskei ha-Rosh* 3:3; Rabbi Yaakov ben Asher, Tur Hoshen Mishpat 4:1; Rabbi Yosef Caro, *Shulhan Arukh:* Hoshen Mishpat 4:1.

20. Rabbi Yaakov ben Asher, *Tur Shulhan Arukh,* Hoshen Mishpat 156:10–11.

21. Rabbi Yosef Colon, *She'elot u-Teshuvot Maharik* 187; also Rabbi Moshe Isserles, *Darkei Moshe,* Hoshen Mishpat 156:9; idem, *Mappah,* Hoshen Mishpat 156:7; Rabbi Moshe Sofer, *She'elot u-Teshuvot Hatam Sofer,* Hoshen Mishpat 44; Rabbi Yehiel Epstein, *Arukh ha-Shulhan,* Hoshen Mishpat 156:13.

22. Rabbi Eliezer Waldenberg, *Ziz Eliezer* 2:23.

23. Rabbi Yosef Ibn Migash, cited in Rabbi Bezalel Ashkenazi, *Shittah Mekubbezet,* Bava Batra 21b; also Rabbi Yaakov ben Asher, *Tur Shulhan Arukh,* Hoshen Mishpat 156:11; Rabbi Moshe Isserles, Hoshen Mishpat 156:7; Rabbi Yehiel Epstein, *Arukh ha-Shulhan,* Hoshen Mishpat 156:11.

24. Rabbi Moshe Feinstein, *Iggerot Moshe,* Hoshen Mishpat 59.

25. Rabbi Abraham Kook, cited in Rabbi Kasriel Tkhursh, "Dinei Shevitot be-Halakhah," pp. 241, 259–261; Shillem Wahrhaftig, *Dinei Avodah BeMishpat Ivrei;* (Tel Aviv: Moreshet, 1969) 981; Rabbi Moshe Feinstein, *Iggerot Moshe,* Hoshen Mishpat 58–599; Rabbi Ovadiah Yosef, *She'elot u-Teshuvot Yehaveh Da'at* 4:48; Rabbi Kasriel Tkhursh, "Dinei Shevitot be-Halakhah," p. 262.

26. Rabbi Moshe Feinstein, *Iggerot Moshe,* Hoshen Mishpat 59.

27. Holly McGammon, "Government by Injunction: The US Judiciary and Strike Action in the Late 19th and Early 20th Centuries," *Work and Occupations* 20, no. 2 (1993): 174–204, idem "Legal Limits on Labor Militancy: Labor Law and the Right to Strike

Since the New Deal," *Social Problems* 37, no. 2 (1990): 206–229; Charles Baird "On Strikers and Their Replacements," *Government Union Review* 12, no. 3 (1991): 1–30 idem "American Union Law: Source of Conflict," *Journal of Labor Research* 11, no. 3 (1990): 269–292; Michael Wallace et al., "American Labor Law: Its Impact on Working Class Militancy," *Social Science History* 12, no. 1 (1988): 1–29.

28. David Dilts, "Privatization of the Public Sector: De Facto Standardization of Labor Law," *Journal of Collective Negotiations in the Public Sector* 24, no. 1 (1995): 37–43; Donald Klinger , "Public Sector Bargaining," *Review of Public Personnel Administration* 13, no. 3 (1993): 19–28.

29. Timothy Koeller, "Union Activity and the Decline in American Trade Union Membership," *Journal of Labor Research* 15, no. 1 (1994): 19–32; Mark Barenberg, "The Political Economy of the Wagner Act: Power, Symbol, and Workplace Cooperation," *Harvard Law Review* 106, no. 7 (1993): 1379–1496; Holly McGammon , "From Repressive Intervention to Integrative Prevention: The US State's Legal Management of Labor Militancy," *Social Forces* 71, no. 3 (1993) 569–601.

8

Faithfully Occupied with
the Public Need

I

A well-known supplication recited in most synagogues each week calls upon the Lord to bless those who are "faithfully occupied" with the needs of the public. In our prayer we ask that He relieve them of hardship and pay them their proper due, an early confirmation that such work is often fraught with difficulty and that the compensation it commands is frequently lower than its counterpart in the private sector.

Given the importance of the public sphere, however, traditional sources go to some lengths in detailing and structuring the role of those who were employed by the Jewish community. We are provided with numerous discussions of propriety, competence, and discretion of communal employees, codified and expanded to meet the needs of other localities. There was an appreciation for the vulnerability of public employees, and

---

Earlier versions of this paper appeared as "An Alternative Source for Contemporary Public Administration: Aspects of Public Service Employment in Classic Jewish Tradition," *Administration and Society* 29, no. 1: 13–17, and "Faithfully Occupied with the Public Need," *Journal of Jewish Communal Service* 74, no. 3: 315–324.

they were extended a degree of security and protection not common in most workplace relationships. At the same time, they often were held to higher standards of accountability and personal conduct, because of the trust and discretion implicit in their office.

As we will demonstrate, their situation, though removed in time, parallels that of public employees and their managers in many industrial societies today. It is surprising, therefore, that aside from occasional references to biblical heroes as precursors to modern leadership, Jewish tradition is rarely employed as a source for contemporary public management or governance.[1] Instead, imperial Rome or the ancient Far East is more commonly invoked as a model for comparative analysis. Yet Jewish sources provide bold contrast in both time and place, spanning some four millennia of recorded history, on several continents, and with numerous iterations of structure, institution, and context.

The interpreters of the tradition operated within diverse social and political systems from ancient Rome to Christian Europe, Moorish Spain, North Africa, and the full expanse of the Arab world. Today they are found primarily in Israel, the United States, and Western Europe. Their text and precedent were rooted in scriptural narrative and talmudic discourse, but they also generated legislative codes, case law, and municipal regulations emerging from Jewish experiments in autonomous self-government, particularly during the medieval period. In addition, contemporaneous writings reflect upon theories of governance and democracy long before Locke and Rousseau, even as they exhibit a keen sense for standards of ethics and propriety among those in positions of leadership.

It is worth noting that the social and political context for Jewish public organization developed in several overlapping phases. The first is discernible in antiquity and early classical times. In this era Jews lived as an independent national entity in their own land, though frequently under the hegemony of an imperial power or in precarious diplomatic balance between two competing empires. To complicate matters further, they had to contend with expatriate populations—ethnic Hebrews living outside the Land of Israel, under foreign rule, yet growing in numbers, wealth, and influence.

An indigenous political and administrative hierarchy emerged, first around a confederation of tribes led by local judges, military leaders, and prophets, followed by a monarchy, priesthood, and centralized religious structure. Despite the auspicious beginnings signaled in the biblical narrative, this was a stormy period marked by violence, civil war, palace intrigue, and internal strife.

In its middle periods, the molders of the tradition were driven from their land, robbed of their national identity, and forced to seek physical survival and cultural continuity where the conditions varied from suspicious isolation to violent hostility. In general, even benign Gentile overlords looked upon Jews as an alien corporate presence best left unto themselves. In large measure their governance, their regulations, and the provision of their services were assigned to their own communal structures almost by default. An excessive royal tax was generally exacted from the community as a whole, in return for its safety under the protection of the local ruler.

In the absence of secular nationalism, the individual had neither a political identity nor any social or legal standing outside his community. Consequently, attempts at public organization among medieval Jews were successful in maintaining control over the lives of adherents through economic, religious, commercial, and social sanctions. At the same time, public leadership, both lay and religious, represented their interests before the local nobility and churchmen, usually through some form of bribery. A loosely aligned network of *kehillot*, or communities, emerged, stretching through Europe, the Mediterranean region, the Near East, and North Africa.[2]

With the advent of more amenable secular polities in the wake of the French Revolution, the influence of the *kehillot* receded. Members of the Jewish community entered the general culture en masse, notably in the United States and Western Europe. The number of loyal adherents was severely curtailed as a result, and the tradition was forced to broaden its scope in response to contemporary challenges. Change was signaled in the emergence of voluntary or associational, rather than corporate, patterns of affiliation, alongside a Jewish national renaissance expressed as political Zionism and the modern State of Israel.[3]

The sum is a vast pool of experience in such arenas of local concern as community development, conflict adjudication, public leadership, and the administration of various services under both normal and adverse conditions. As a result of this diverse history, the arbiters of the tradition, those empowered to interpret its sources and apply them to contemporaneous circumstances, often inferred and extrapolated from references and precedents far removed from the issues at hand. For example, they adduced principles of leadership and of public employment from biblical and talmudic descriptions of the Israelite king or high priest, institutions that both had long since passed from the scene. Similarly, rulings about job security were inferred from texts dealing with battlefield commissions and hereditary peerage. The same process inevitably determines applications to modern conditions.

What follows is a detailed attempt to mine the traditional sources for what they may tell us about several aspects of public employment, particularly tenure and job security, collective organization in the public sector, accountability for quality assurance, and the ethical parameters of public management. The closing section will consider themes in common with American administrative practice and make appropriate comparative inferences.

II

Jewish sources severely limit the discretion of public authorities over the renewal of employment contracts. The Talmud (e.g., Yoma 12b and 73a) explains that temporary or emergency commissions were often awarded to the priestly leaders of ancient Israel. While these might expire in time, many of the prerogatives and honors attached to the office were retained.

As Maimonides explains: "We increase from a position of authority, and we do not reduce to a lower authority, for holiness is upgraded and not lowered. And we never remove one from a position of authority in Israel unless he has offended."[4] This ruling is of interest on several grounds. First, it suggests an element of the sacred in the public service, analogous to the priesthood. Indeed at its source, the Hebrew word for "priest" (*kohen*) means "one who serves," and those entrusted with the welfare of the people carry a special trust. Maimonides appears to postulate an early tenure provision for those in "a position of authority," based on the code of holiness at the core of public service. The theme runs as a thread throughout his writings on the topic.

Elsewhere, Maimonides upholds and extends this ruling in a direct petition regarding a public functionary against whom suspicions of malfeasance had been raised.[5] If the charges are substantiated, he reasons, the official surely should be penalized, but then he must be returned to his post, "for we do not remove one from the holy." It is noteworthy that the official in this case performed no sacerdotal functions, but was a member of the communal board. Evidently, this sacred trust was implicit in the secular public service, not just the priesthood. It adhered to mundane administrative functions and was not reserved for the Temple ritual with which priests were most commonly associated.

Other authorities concurred, but they rooted their support for public service job security in different considerations.[6] Rather than the priesthood of ancient Israel, they invoked a talmudic passage (Gittin 60b) regarding reverence for established tradition. There we are taught that if a certain household was customarily used for some public function, the venue should not be changed summarily. Concern for good neighborly relations and the "pathways of peace" demand that we protect this household from the untoward suspicion and gossip inevitably raised by a sudden change in policy.

By analogy, it was argued that we must express similar concern for the reputation of public employees. Summary removal would raise suspicion about their competence or integrity, especially if no term of employment had been previously stipulated. Unless malfeasance could be proven, they should be secure in their positions and their employment should continue indefinitely.

However, removing the sanctity of public service as a prop allowed the force of local custom to undo these early tenure provisions. Thus,

> In our age, it is the custom to appoint people over the public need for a time. When that time elapses, they leave and others enter in their place. . . whether they receive a salary or not,

and even if no term was set for them. . . . Since the custom is to change, concern about suspicion disappears. The pure have for generations borne the public burden and then have left and others replaced them.[7]

As an aside, it is noteworthy that this ruling makes no distinction between professional and voluntary employees. However the position is assigned, rotation in office is looked upon as a healthy concomitant to vibrant administration. All are expected to vacate their positions upon completion of their term. Later authorities confirmed this ruling, especially in regard to civil rather than ecclesiastical appointments.[8]

Nevertheless, strong sentiment in support of tenure provisions persisted. More recently, the license to dismiss public employees absent cause has been blunted. Leading modern thinkers, including Rabbi Yisroel Meir Kagan and Rabbi Moshe Feinstein, ruled that, custom to the contrary notwithstanding, public employees should not be dismissed except for cause, even at the expiration of a stipulated term of service. The reasoning includes broad concern for equity, the financial well-being of the employee, and a general sense that contracts of service are normally renewed.[9]

Nevertheless, special consideration also may be due the public authority. For an example, employees have no claim to tenure if the demand for their service no longer exists, or if they can be shown to have clearly waived their tenure rights at the time of their hire. Similarly, if the employee in question is a front-line worker or of little authority, and if the decision to dismiss is routine and no mark of controversy is attached, then he may not merit special protection or job security.[10]

Jewish tradition also looks upon civic appointment as a form of peerage or royal commission, analogous to the sanctity of the public trust. As such, an office may pass by order of succession similar to any other inheritance. Rather than the high priest, here it was the monarch who was invoked as precedent and model. Scripture binds the king of Israel to the ways of the Lord, "so that he have many years in his monarchy, he and his children in the midst of Israel" (Deuteronomy 17:20). From the concluding phrase, Maimonides rules that "all authority and all appointments in Israel are an inheritance to children and to their children forever."[11]

Yet succession was by no means automatic. In the Talmud (e.g., Ketubbot 103b) the principle is qualified by character and competence, with the former given precedence. Apparently it was assumed that competence may be learned more easily than character. Community sensibilities and long-established custom may also mitigate a specific appointment.[12] Vocational succession later expanded beyond the limits common in material inheritance, to which children normally acceded only upon a parent's death. Here they may be appointed during the lifetime of a parent or to assist in cases of illness or advanced age. Further, they may also assume full responsibility if a parent suffers total incapacity.[13]

III

As we have noted, those responsible for Jewish labor regulations were much concerned to maintain and expand the freedom and discretion of full-time workers, lest they be so beholden to their employers as to become virtually indentured. Under limited circumstances, therefore, the Talmud provides workers with the right to rescind contractual relationships even "in midday" (Bava Kamma 116b, Bava Metzia 10a). Of course, compensation might be due the employer for damage and loss of income. Still, the laborer's freedom of action was to be upheld.

In the case of a public employee, however, these concerns were relaxed in the face of the overriding public interest, similar to labor actions in critical industries, noted above. A talmudic source tells us, for example, that it may be necessary to limit the freedom of those in the public employ who provide essential services. Thus if "the time of the festival draws near, and he would leave for his home, we may restrain his hand until he appoints another in his place" (Tosefta Bava Metzia 11:13). While the ruling did not uniformly find its way into the mainstream of Jewish legal thought, it is cited by at least one leading medieval authority, Rabbi Shmuel ben Adret.[14]

Other Jewish thinkers also held public employees to higher standards of quality and accountability than those in the private sector. Consider the following from Maimonides:

> One who gardens for the state and causes loss, a butcher of the municipality who spoiled meat, a bloodletter who injured, a scribe who voided documents, and a teacher who was negligent with children and taught them not, or taught them in error, and all other such professionals who cause irretrievable loss are to be summarily dismissed. They stand as forewarned to be cautious in their work, for the public has ordained that they be appointed over them.[15]

Several points of contention exercised the commentaries to Maimonides here. They ascribe his thinking to the talmudic precedent in the case of Runia, a gardener who issued a grievance against his dismissal for cause (Bava Metzia 109a, Bava Batra 21b). Maimonides offers no definition of "irretrievable loss" or of its application, and his supporters find it hard to demonstrate that the instances he lists are examples of loss that cannot be compensated.

They argue, for example, that children taught in error must "unlearn" before they can learn correctly, and the loss of their time or opportunity cannot be retrieved. Similarly, pain may be compensated, but good health cannot be retrieved, and a householder in need of victuals is poorly served by monetary recompense for meat that was spoiled.[16]

The call for summary dismissal of these workers puzzles them still more. The case of Runia in the Talmud makes no distinction between public and private employment. The analysis is grounded in a dispute over negligence in what appears to be a privately contracted service. The legal question turns on the type of damage incurred. Workers who cause irretrievable loss, it concludes, may be dismissed without warning. The nature of their work requires that they be more fastidious. It is Maimonides who adds that such negligence is cause for summary dismissal only in the public sector as a function of the trust invested by the citizenry.

The point is hotly contested. Interlocutors reject the distinction between public and private employees, preferring a literal understanding of the talmudic passage and staking a powerful claim for employee accountability in the process.[17] Yet Maimonides is not alone. His supporters, primarily Rabbi Yosef Caro, explain that a superficial reading of the Runia case is misleading. The grievance at issue was lodged not against a private employer, but against either a municipal administrator or a private citizen petitioning for the dismissal of a communal employee. In either case, Runia was not a private contractor but a public employee. Maimonides is correct in concluding, therefore, that the scope of this judgment does not extend beyond the public sector.[18]

Subsequent adjudication has blunted many aspects of the debate and sharpened others. For example, later authorities suggest that, regardless of context, dismissal without warning may be in order only for those with a history of negligence, defined by at least three prior offenses. They extend this to pro bono services. Incompetent volunteers, meaning those who habitually cause irretrievable damage, also may be summarily removed from office.

Finally, public servants are held to higher standards of accountability in yet another area of their employ. Dismissal from privately contracted services or from a job in the commercial sector need not carry decertification or prevent the worker from employment elsewhere. Yet dismissal from public service for irretrievable damage, as described above, may carry automatic suspension of license and severe limitations on future public employment in the same field.[19]

IV

Jewish texts deal extensively with the high personal standards of behavior and propriety demanded of those in the communal service. Such individuals were to look upon their positions with reverence and treat their constituents with the utmost respect and deference. In particular there was concern about the indiscriminate use of *serarah*, authority or influence that could easily become willful and arrogant. Based on several talmudic anecdotes (Rosh Hashanah 17a, Sanhedrin 7b, Kiddushin 70a), Maimonides rules:

> An individual may never act with *serarah* over the community, nor in a boorish spirit, but rather with humility and awe. . . . Nor may he make light of them even though they be ignorant. Nor may he walk on their heads, even if they be simple and lowly, for they are the children of Abraham, Isaac, and Jacob. . . . He must patiently carry the demands of the public even as did our master Moses. [20]

Note that Maimonides rests this view, not upon specific transactions with one constituent or another, but on the mission represented in communal service generally, linked to the biblical history of the Jewish people and their glorious ancestry. Later he warns administrators against public intoxication and frivolous behavior, admonishing them never to instill "fear that is not for the sake of heaven." A later authority would rule that long sufferance was in order among communal employees, even should their constituents "curse them and stone them."[21]

The rabbis were equally taken with matters of administrative discretion and confidentiality. They were well aware of the broad scriptural exhortations against tale-bearing, rumor-mongering, and slander, ethical principles especially salient in the dense social environment of medieval Jewish life. They appreciated that communal service provided access to sensitive information, the public exposure of which could be damaging even in the absence of malice. Juridical ethics and procedure became the model for behavior here, as communal decisions were considered quasi-judicial and carried the power of law.

For example, talmudic sources (Sanhedrin 29–31) find that once a decision is reached, it would be inappropriate for a judge to tell a litigant: "I supported you but my colleagues opposed, and what could I do, since they were in the majority." In codifying this principle, Maimonides cites a talmudic anecdote in which a scholar was ejected from the study hall for revealing privileged information classified over twenty years earlier. He rules that even the written text of a decision must be handed down anonymously. Only general reference to a dissent was permissible, in deference to concerns that a misimpression of unanimity violated the demands of simple honesty and candor.[22]

A consistent stream of rabbinic thought was discomforted by such rigorous confidentiality, however. There was fear that it might limit the opportunity for redress from erroneous decisions and further contribute to administrative arrogance and abuse. If individual members of a judiciary or, by implication, of a community board or arbitration panel saw good legal cause for reversing the decisions of the majority, were they not duty bound at least to inform the interested parties?

Later rulings accommodated this concern. Dissenters were enjoined from actively soliciting and organizing community opposition to judicial or administrative rulings. However, they could respond to further inquiries and seek a reversal if (1) the substance of their dissent was in clear reaction to a misinterpretation of the law and not purely a matter of opinion and judgment, (2) they were unsuccessful in correcting the injustice through discrete communication with their colleagues, and (3) there was an available avenue of compensation for the aggrieved.[23]

Finally, the rabbis were most insistent about the need to avoid conflicts of interest among those entrusted with public funds. The rules regarding charity administrators and their agents are an apt example of the lengths to which the talmudic authorities would go to avoid even the appearance of impropriety. A well-known talmudic passage tells us:

> The charity fund is collected by two . . . because we do not place *serarah* upon the community, but with two . . . charity collectors may never separate from each other. . . . If one finds money [while on duty], he should not place it in his purse but put it into the charity box and later remove it at home. Similarly, if one is repaid a debt [while on duty], he should not place it in his purse but put it into the charity box and later remove it at home.
>
> (Bava Batra 8–9)

Once collected, all coins must be recorded "one-by-one," to ensure the honesty of the count. Once distributions to the poor are completed, overages of funds or goods may be transferred or sold. However, administrators and their agents may not be party to any such transaction because of the potential conflict that may ensue. As tribute to the trust they enjoyed, the Talmud concludes, "We do not audit collectors of charity" for the moneys entrusted to them. Though the entire passage was later codified almost verbatim, one authority suggests that the wise administrator will voluntarily submit to a periodic audit.[24]

Later thinkers demanded a public accounting, however, especially if (1) a question had been raised about the expenditure of funds, (2) the administrators were paid professionals, or (3) doing so had become the local custom. In all events, the accounting was a discrete affair, entrusted to a small committee and attached to a standard review, rather than a random investigation.[25]

Medieval authorities also demanded that contributors take responsibility for their munificence. They were expected to exert themselves to ensure that moneys collected on behalf of charity were handled honestly. Thus in discussing the higher levels of charitable giving, Maimonides encourages support for a community fund as an anonymous intermediary between donor and recipient. However, he rules, "a person shall not contribute to a charity fund unless he knows that the appointee [over the fund] is honest, wise, and straight, as was Rabbi Hananiah ben Teradyon."[26]

The reference is curious. Talmudic anecdote records that Rabbi Hananiah ben Teradyon was indeed a local charity administrator (Avodah Zarah 17b). In this position, he was responsible for several accounts, including a designated fund for distribution only as part of the Purim celebration. The commentaries differ on the details, but he apparently confused this fund with another or with his own money. In either case, he made good on the shortfall at his own expense and in a manner that embarrassed neither the recipient nor the donor. He is held aloft as a model, therefore, less for administrative competence than for exemplary personal integrity.

Later thinkers averred that in the absence of a person of such stature, it would be best to seek out one who was "wise in the ways of collection."[27] Tragically, much of the discussion surrounding Rabbi Hananiah as a model of charitable administration has been mooted by history. Today he is known neither for his honesty nor for his competence as a public servant. He is remembered, instead, for the torture that led to his murder, suffering among the Ten Martyrs of Rome memorialized in the Yom Kippur prayer service.

V

These classic sources allow specific inferences and contrasts that are relevant to modern applications. Conflicts in contemporary public management have their analogues in very different societies over a period of some two millennia. Social, political, and technological change notwithstanding, concerns for quality and productivity, tenure and continuity in office, ethics and administrative accountability, survive the centuries and retain much of their former edge.

Consider job security as an example. In the United States, tenure provisions were largely based upon the concerns of early reformers about partisanship and the independence of the civil service. Absent such protection, public employees would be subject to untoward political pressure by elected officials and influential constituents. They would become embroiled in partisan battles, rendering independent administrative judgment impossible.

Today, such provisions have come under fire. Critics claim that rather than buffer public employees from partisanship, tenure rules have insulated them from managerial influence and accountability, and made them unresponsive to the needs of their clients. As a result, elected and appointed public executives have precious little discretion over the performance of their subordinates and lack the control needed to fulfill the missions for which they will be evaluated. Rather than independence of thought and action, tenure provisions are said to contribute to sloth and arrogance.

In contrast with the cynicism that often surrounds contemporary civil employment, consider the tone struck by Maimonides. For him, public service is a sacred commission, part nobility and part priesthood, reminiscent of the noblesse oblige that informs public leadership in other traditions. An important part of early political culture in the United States, it is implicit in recent attempts to derive a "calling" in modern public service.[28]

For Maimonides, job security and protection are the natural concomitants of this view of public service. Absent proof of malfeasance, it would be as unthinkable to remove these perquisites from any public office as it would be from the royal house. To do so would undermine social authority, along with respect for the deity in which it was grounded. In his words, "we do not remove one from the holy, whether in the highest court or in the local congregation," and "we do not reduce to a lower authority, for holiness is upgraded and not lowered."

Even among those who do not share his vision, consideration is given to the good name of public employees. To remove them, even at term, raises questions about their competence or their honesty, demeaning them and their options for future employment. Only when concerns for personal reputation are blunted by local practice may tenure provisions be relaxed. Quoth Ben-Adret: "Since the custom is to change, suspicion has disappeared." The message is clear, therefore, to those who would limit the reach of tenure provisions or eliminate them altogether. To do so is to undermine the essence of the public trust and the good name of those employed within it. Instead, it behooves educators, practitioners, and employers in the field to revive a sense of the sacred (or its secular equivalent) as a vital part of the mission and the core of the profession.

So, too, for those who would restrict the rights of public employees to organize or to engage in strikes and job actions. New York's Taylor Law and similar legislation elsewhere notwithstanding, members of the "Jewish civil service" are not to be treated differently from private employees. They are endowed equally with the freedom to set standards for wages, working conditions, and mutual security. It also appears unnecessary for them to organize separately from the private sector, obviating the need for civil employee federations and permitting them to join with their fellows in private industry.

The thrust of the tradition suggests that the right to strike is curtailed only in cases of overriding public interest or civil emergency. Then, restrictions are imposed by industry, regardless of auspices or jurisdiction. Thus teachers, health professionals, employees of energy installations, and the like, may be enjoined from striking, or their disputes may be relegated to binding arbitration without interruption of service, whether they are employed by the public authority or by private or non-governmental organizations.

Notwithstanding the leeway extended to civil employees, they are to be held strictly accountable for their performance.

Regarding quality of service, Maimonides' demand that communal employees be held to higher standards of productivity and competence has a notably modern ring, thus: "the public has ordained that they be appointed over them." The point is a natural outgrowth of his vision of their role as sacred, and of the calling and the trust it implies. The public may be obliged to protect the security and the good name of its employees, to allow them to organize and regulate themselves. Still, the trust with which they are "ordained" obliges them to take care that they cause no harm. Those who hold this commission will be strictly accountable for their performance and for their expertise. They are "forewarned" and may suffer summary dismissal and decertification.

Medieval interlocutors submit that the emphasis upon quality should not be restricted to the public service. A similar trust exists in the relationship between workers and any employer. They should be equally accountable for the quality of their work. The point runs contrary to the contemporary cynicism about productivity and quality in the public sector. In this formulation, public employees serve as the model, the standard against which accountability is to be measured. The debate hinges on whether private employers have the right to make equally stringent demands upon their workers or whether they cannot be held accountable for similar lapses in competence.

Finally, the standards of ethical behavior demanded of communal servants are a natural extension of this vision. In seeking to protect the integrity and unanimity of public authority, Jewish tradition takes a dim view of those who would sensationalize internal disputes and controversies, exploiting them for personal gain. There was a deep appreciation for discretion regarding classified information, lest officials violate their bond by indulging in tale-bearing or gossip. Most especially, any appearance of impropriety or conflict of interest is to be avoided among those entrusted with public resources.

They must be above reproach, avoiding untoward transactions with the funds at their disposal. As the practice unfolded, they were called upon to provide a careful accounting of income and allocations. As reciprocal, donors and philanthropists were duty-bound to investigate the institutions on which they endowed their munificence. It was their obligation to ensure that the administrators were honest and straightforward conservators of the public weal.

1. See, e.g. Steven Brams, *Biblical Games: A Strategic Analysis of Stories in the Old Testament* (Cambridge, Mass.: MIT Press, 1980); Michael Walzer, *Exodus and Revolution* (New York: Basic Books, 1986); Aaron Wildavsky, *The Nursing Father: Moses as Political Leader* (Tuscaloosa: University of Alabama Press, 1984); idem, *Assimilation vs. Separation: Joseph the Administrator and the Politics of Religion in Biblical Israel* (New Brunswick, N.J.: Transaction, 1992).

2. Stuart Cohen, *The Three Crowns: Structures of Communal Discourse in Early Rabbinic Society* (Oxford: Cambridge University Press, 1990); Daniel Elazar, *Kinship and Consent: The Jewish Political Tradition and Its Contemporary Uses* (Lanham, Md.: University of America Press, 1983); idem, *The Jewish Polity: Jewish Political Organization from Biblical Times to the Present* (Bloomington: Indiana University Press, 1985).

3. See Henry Feingold, *Zion in America: The Jewish Experience from Colonial Times to the Present* (New York: Hippocrene, 1974); Stanley Feldstein, *The Land That I Show You: Three Centuries of Jewish Life in America* (New York: Doubleday, 1978); Arthur Hertzberg, *The Zionist Idea* (New York: Atheneum, 1973); Howard Sachar, *The Course of Modern Jewish History* (New York: Delta, 1958).

4. Rabbi Moshe Maimonides, *Yad ha-Hazakah*, Hilkhot Kelei ha-Mikdash 4:21.

5. Rabbi Moshe Maimonides, *Teshuvot ha-Rambam* 111.

6. Rabbi Yom Tov Ishbili, *Hiddushei ha-Ritva*, Makkot 13a; Rabbi Yosef Caro, *Beit Yosef*, Orah Hayyim 53.

7. Rabbi Shmuel ben Adret, *She'elot u-Teshuvot ha-Rashba* 5:283.

8. E.g., Rabbi Yosef Caro, *Shulhan Arukh*, Orah Hayyim 53:26; Rabbi Yehiel Michael Epstein, *Arukh ha-Shulhan*, Orah Hayyim 53:26; Rabbi Elijah of Vilna, Orah Hayyim 53:26.

9. Rabbi Yisrael Meir Ha-Kohen, *Mishnah Berurah* 53:86; Rabbi Moshe Feinstein, *Iggerot Moshe*, Hoshen Mishpat 77.

10. J. David Bleich, *Contemporary Halachic Problems* (New York: Yeshiva University Press, 1977), pp. 189–194; Aaron Levine, *Free Enterprise and Jewish Law* (New York: Ktav, 1980), pp. 52–55; Shillem Wahrhaftig, *Dinei Avodah be-Mishpat Ivri* (Tel Aviv: Moreshet, 1969), 1:240–241; Rabbi Eliezer Waldenberg, *Ziz Eliezer* 3:29.

11. Rabbi Moshe Maimonides, *Yad*, Hilkhot Shoftim 1:7, Hilkhot Kelei ha-Mikdash 4:20.

12. Rabbi Yosef Caro, *Kesef Mishneh*, Kelei ha-Mikdash 4:20; Rabbi Shmuel ben Adret, *She'elot u-Teshuvot ha-Rashba* 1:300; Rabbi Moshe Isserles, *Mappah*, Yoreh De'ah 245:22

13. Rabbi Moshe Isserles, *Mappah*, Orah Hayyim 53:25; Rabbi Israel Meir Ha-Kohen, *Mishnah Berurah* 53:83–84.

14. Rabbi Shmuel ben Adret, *Hiddushei ha-Rashba*: Bava Batra 9a.

15. Rabbi Moshe Maimonides, *Yad*, Hilkhot Sekhirut 10:7.

16. E.g., Rabbi Vidal of Tolosa, *Maggid Mishneh*, Sekhirut 10:7; Tosafot to Bava Batra 21a.

17. Rabbi Avraham ibn-Daud, *Hassagot ha-Ravad*, Sekhirut 10:7; Rabbi Yaakov ben Asher, *Tur Shulhan Arukh*, Hoshen Mishpat 306:12; Rabbi Yoel Sirkes, *Hiddushei ha-Bah*, Hoshen Mishpat 306:12; Rabbi Moshe Isserles, *Mappah*, Hoshen Mishpat 306:12.

18. Rabbi Yosef Caro, *Shulhan Arukh*, Hoshen Mishpat 306:12; Rabbi Yosef Caro, *Beit Yosef*, Hoshen Mishpat 306:12.

19. Rabbi Vidal of Tolosa, *Maggid Mishneh*, Sekhirut 10:7; Rabbi Joshua Falk-Katz, *Sefer Me'irat Einayim* 306:20; Rabbi Moshe Isserles, *Mappah*, Hoshen Mishpat 306:8; Rabbi Yehiel Epstein, *Arukh ha-Shulhan*, Hoshen Mishpat 306:16.

20. Rabbi Moshe Maimonides, *Yad*, Hilkhot Sanhedrin 25:1–2.

21. Rabbi Yaakov ben Asher, *Tur Shulhan Arukh*, Hoshen Mishpat 8:12.

22. Rabbi Moshe Maimonides, *Yad*, Hilkhot Sanhedrin 22:7–8; see also Rabbi Yosef Caro, *Shulhan Arukh*, Hoshen Mishpat 19:1–2.

23. Rabbi Avraham Eisenstadt, *Pithei Teshuvah*, Hoshen Mishpat 19:1.

24. Rabbi Moshe Maimonides, *Yad*, Hilkhot Mattanot Einayim 9:8–11; Rabbi Yaakov ben Asher, *Tur Shulhan Arukh*, Yoreh De'ah 257:3; Rabbi Moshe Isserles, 1965, *Mappah*, Hoshen Mishpat 257:2.

25. Rabbi Yehiel Michael Epstein, *Arukh ha-Shulhan*, Yoreh De'ah 257: 12; Rabbi Moshe Isserles, *Mappah*, Yoreh De'ah 257:2; Rabbi Shabbetai ben Meir Ha-Kohen, *Siftei Kohen*, Yoreh De'ah 257:3.

26. Rabbi Moshe Maimonides, *Yad*, Hilkhot Mattanot Amyim 10:8.

27. Rabbi Yosef Caro, *Bet Yosef*, Yoreh De'ah 259:12; Rabbi David ibn Zimra, *Hilkhot Mattanot Amyim* 10:8; Tosafot to Bava Batra 10a.

28. See, e.g., Philip Schor, "Public Service as a Calling: An Exploration of a Concept, Part II," *International Journal of Public Administration* 13, no. 5 (1990): 649–691.

9

By the Sweat of Your Brow

I

Summarizing and evaluating our exploration of Jewish attitudes toward work and the workplace is no simple matter. Jewish thought encompasses divergent streams and traditions often forged under circumstances that made mere survival the primary objective. The tradition encompasses a broad stream of experience and reflection, intermingled with behavior and practice, and underscored by often-unspoken assumptions and verities. More a literature or a culture than a singular ideology, many themes are surrounded by an array of postures and positions.

Originally built on a theological commitment to revelation, the tradition has been elaborated, expanded, and discovered over the millennia to meet the demands of diverse needs and opportunities. Though separated by centuries and continents, these often live in uneasy intellectual tension or indifference, one with the next. The mainstream must wrestle with minority positions that hold sway as circumstances conspire. Prooftext and precedent may be found to support a mutually exclusive complex of values or customs, any of which may be marshaled, or easily mistaken for normative practice.

Moreover, economic activity generally and labor legislation specifically are the modal expressions by which contemporaneous practice and prevailing external, secular, and non-Jewish custom have been introduced as normative models for legislation and policy. Devised as an easement for Jewish commercial interests, this elasticity often makes it difficult to discern that which is an original part of the tradition and that which has been insinuated from without. Alternatively, the very notion of its insinuation cannot be separated from the tradition itself.

The Jewish outlook on work and on the relationship between the worker and his employer serves as a primary example of this diversity of opinion and behavior. As we have demonstrated, some see labor as a scourge and an evil, imposed upon mankind for its willful disobedience. For others, work is the "way of the world," compared to the love of one's mate and even to life itself. Some warn parents that to neglect vocational training in the rearing of a child is to raise him as a thief and brigand. By contrast, some would have the child study nothing but the word of God, with the promise that others will perform his labors. One involved in Torah and its study ought not to be distracted by the toils and travails of the marketplace, they aver, while their interlocutors claim that Torah study not merged with gainful employment will come to naught. To allow religious devotion to force dependence upon public support is to demean the Torah and place one's eternal reward in jeopardy.

Still, this much can be said. Even those who celebrate labor and see its great religious and social value maintain that work must never become an obsession, the organizing principle of life. The accumulation of wealth is no sin, but Weber-cum-Calvin notwithstanding, neither is it a modality by which righteousness is evaluated. The rewards of vocation are temporary. Each bears the seeds of its own decline, providing precious little security in old age. Therefore, in teaching the child a trade, one is advised to guide him toward a livelihood that is simple and clean, one that will overtax neither his energy nor his integrity.

Nor may profession be employed as the primary molder of personal identity. Whether for material benefit or personal fulfillment, the demands of the workplace easily isolate one from all activities except those that provide financial reward or career advancement. Divorced from significant social contact outside, the shop or office comes to replace social and religious community, while professional collegiality stands instead of personal relationships.

To this, Jewish thought stands categorically opposed. Significance, permanence, and fulfillment are to be found outside the workplace, through Torah, defined by study, prayer, and personal or collective acts of kindness, empathic behavior, probity, and compassion. Here one reaches his full potential, better integrating his life and, in the process, helping himself to succeed on the job as well.

The point is clearly reflected in the Jewish formula for financial success. Hard work figures handily, to be sure, but only alongside honesty and integrity, the first of the divine standards of righteousness. Yet all this must be matched by merit, understood not as market value but as personal morality. Good deeds, prayer, contemplation, and study are parts of the mix in a faith that is integrative and holistic rather than fragmentary. Much is relegated to human initiative. Yet there is a stark recognition that some portion of success resides far beyond human control. Luck, fate, destiny or simply *mazal* may be a controlling factor at any time. Here there is little chance for mastery save by supplications to the Lord and an abiding faith in His just means.

This is meant to heighten understanding and compassion for those who reside at a lesser social station, such as one's employees. Their human dignity transcends their status, for at base, each is a servant to no one but the Lord alone. Moreover, an employer may ill-ignore the common heritage and ancestry that binds him to his workers. Each is a scion of nobility, child of the founders of the nation and its faith. Communal links that augur collective memory, a shared fate, and a common destiny stand higher than differences of social or economic caste, which, in any event, are seen as superficial and transitory.

Yet there is more to appreciating that a goodly portion of success stems from the munificence of the Lord along with, according to many talmudic sages, a serendipitous confluence of the stars. Surely, the legitimacy of wealth and private property is never seriously in question. Still, here one becomes less an owner with free rein over his holdings then a conservator bound by commitments and obligations. The charge is to employ personal resources in improving the universe, for it is by that bar that accountability will be measured. Personal worth will be calculated less by what was accumulated and more by how it contributed to the common good.

Further, economic need is no moral flaw, the mark of the accursed. Nor is it necessarily rooted in personal weakness, inefficiency, or torpor. Many of the most distinguished sages and saints were laborers, while still others suffered life-long poverty. Rather, prosperity is often cyclical. Economic downturns put captains of industry into the debt and employ of others forthwith. It is a point worthy of consideration by the owners of wealth as they regard their employees as well as any others who depend upon them or petition for their assistance.

From public assistance and social welfare to demands for compassion and charity in the workplace, Jewish tradition places a web of obligations on the individual and on society to seek after the safety and security of the whole, but especially of those most vulnerable. Of course, the beneficiaries of such compassion, in our case employees, are adjured to work with single-minded energy and personal commitment, giving priority to the quality and the integrity of their craft. Yet this is no quid pro quo. Each side fulfills its obligation almost apart from the behavior of the other, even as the tradition ever bends toward the weak.

II

Yet there is an inherent danger in such bias. Much has been written of late about the emergence of a "culture of entitlement" in modern industrial economies.[1] Workers, it is claimed, become so accustomed to the myriad benefits and supports mandated by law and customary business practice that they soon come to see them as natural rights to which they are inherently entitled. This is matched by a chorus of victimization wherein various groups justify their entitlement by demonstrating that they have been injured, personally or collectively, by the ills of a society or the malice of its citizens. Competition becomes fierce among rival interests seeking to demonstrate how the disadvantages of others pale by comparison to their own or to those of their forebears in some prior historical period. The goal is to garner the valued status of "protected minority" along with the complex of social and economic benefits that accrue with such designation.

In all this, little consideration is afforded the spiraling price to employers and the impact upon the economy broadly. Over the past few decades, rising labor costs and the resultant loss in productivity have been among the primary roots of business downturn in the West. Outsourcing to foreign contractors with access to cheaper pools of labor has been a natural result, especially in traditional "smokestack" industries, hastening the shift to service-based enterprise and an increased reliance on high technology. In the not too long run, both trends come back to haunt labor in the form of cutbacks, reductions in employment, and foreign competition, even as they impact negatively upon industry and force changes in the economy generally.

In its predisposition for the needs of the worker, Jewish practice did not anticipate such eventualities, staked as they are to the vagaries of modern economics. Indeed, the emphasis on *minhag*, prevailing business practice, as an important base for the development of tradition in this arena means that advances in the cause of labor enter the corpus of Jewish practice, inter alia, and almost without regard to their effect upon the broader economy. The Jewish posture toward employee relations must remain ever beholden to its environment, scars, pocks, and all.

Still, there may be some palliative in its insistence that both parties to a labor contract are bound not purely by their connection to each other but by the their obligation to do right and justly before the Lord. Thus the benefits due a worker should never be misinterpreted as privileges and entitlements that inhere in his position or in the disabilities he has suffered. They are obligations upon his employer that transcend their contract, even as they bind their relationship. Indeed, the call for compassion beyond the letter of the law, alongside various other extralegal remedies attached to Jewish economic thought, emerges from much the same impulse.

This emphasis upon the obligations of the one rather than the rights of the other, upon the sanctity of the relationship rather than the autonomy of its parties, gives their contract almost a religious quality. At the least, it may militate against either party's seeing his prerogatives and gains as entitlements. Rather, they are obligations placed upon the other by virtue of his fealty to the Lord, circumscribed more by claims of justice and propriety than by the demands of commerce and finance. They are part of a much broader network of such obligations, religious and secular, moral and social, ecclesiastical and civil, that bolster a faith in action. The intent is equity and reciprocity. The mission is to cement vital social relationships and perpetuate the people and their faith.

These points also are evident in what is glaringly absent in Jewish economic theory. As we have demonstrated, concern for the worker is grounded in his vulnerability and encumbrance. Even if he is financially able, employers must treat him kindly. He "sets his spirit" to the job and its wage; that is, he risks injury and loss to fulfill the demands placed upon him by his employer. His financial condition aside, this qualification is sufficient.

Still, there is no doubt wherein the discretion and the prerogative of ownership reside. Nowhere in Jewish thought is the employee ethically or legally empowered to share in the initiation of policy, to participate in the distribution of capital, or to partake in the allocation of resources. Nor is there much support for this even as a sound management principal. Stakeholder theory notwithstanding, it is difficult to find in Jewish tradition a primary commitment to the worker that competes with the fiduciary relationship at the core of managerial obligations to investors, stockholders, or the demands of profit. Here the responsibilities of the conservator that attend ownership stop short.

III

A quick glance at other Western religious traditions as they grapple with the ethical concerns of the modern workplace may help elucidate our point. Consider, for an example, the directions forged by Catholic thinkers for much of the nineteenth century. Papal authority formally entered the realm of modern economic thought with the publication of *Rerum Novarum* in 1891. Authored by Pope Leo XIII, the encyclical was intended to help ameliorate the condition of poor workers due to capitalist excesses. It ushered a new era of church activism, later to be dubbed Catholic social teaching.

This effort paralleled Jewish thought as we have considered it thus far. Leo XIII grounded workplace relationships in the inherent dignity of the laborer, in a concern for the common good, and in the reciprocal obligation for employees to work energetically and honestly. It also added the welfare of the worker's family as an important dimension in any calculation of wages, benefits, or career advancement.[2]

However, this was soon followed by a series of pronouncements that presumed the employee's role as a partner in the enterprise from which he would achieve his God-ordained rights to human fulfillment. From Pius XI (1922–39) to John XXIII (1958–63) to John Paul II (1978–), encyclicals, letters, and homilies have made this a central point of Catholic social policy. Employers are obligated to expand the role of their workers, encourage their participation in all facets of business, and develop in them the professional and technical skills that will support their new and activist role. As early as 1949 the National Catholic Convention of the newly created Republic of West Germany demanded workers' rights of "co-determination." Defined as "a natural right according to the order laid down by God," this would have extended employee involvement from the day-to-day activities of the firm to its most fundamental strategic decisions.

It should be noted that Pope Pius XII (1939–58) took strong exception to these trends. He evidently concurred with the proposition that employers bear an obligation to consider the personal and social needs of their workers. Yet he saw nothing in Catholic tradition to justify the restrictions and limitations of ownership implicit in co-determinism and the contemporaneous movements of worker participation. Never formally presented as an encyclical, his was a minority opinion among the many churchmen with views more liberal and expansive.[3]

As we have noted, this contrasts sharply with the classic attitudes of Calvinist thought as interpreted by Weber and his disciples. Here the role of entrepreneur took primacy, while the worker, alongside the disadvantaged and the poor, deserves little support. For the deeply religious, the Lord had ordained their depressed status and their low prospects for financial success. For the more secular, their travail was based in the weakness of their character and the paucity of their merit. To paraphrase one analyst, Calvin did for the bourgeoisie what Marx did for the proletariat.[4]

Somewhat predictably, Jewish tradition falls part-way between. Employers are expected to treat their workers kindly. They must look upon them with empathic understanding, paying their wages punctually, overlooking occasional lapses in the quality of their effort, and allowing them to organize in pursuit of their best interests. However, there is little doctrinal basis for the mandate of empowerment or for the participatory managerial style implicit in recent papal pronouncements. There is no requirement to obscure differences of status on the job by inviting workers to join in managerial decision-making.

Aside from a respect for ownership and property, the silence of Jewish sources about these new labor initiatives is based on another intellectual premise as well. Catholic social teaching, as reflected in these recent encyclicals, has increasingly come to emphasize work as a source of moral and social achievement for the laborer and the workplace, a venue for him to perfect his dignity and his humanity. Consequently, it is natural to encourage workers to develop their personal and professional potential on the job, and it is natural that they actively participate in making the decisions that affect them.

As we have noted, Jewish sources discern an intrinsic religious significance in labor. By the honest execution of a trade, one protects his own good name and even emulates the Lord. Still, the seeds of religious fulfillment lie elsewhere. One reaches his potential and finds his humanity in study, prayer, penitence, and good deeds, wherein the venue is family, the synagogue, the study hall, and the institutions of community. The empowerment of workers may promote productivity, reduce grievances, and make for good employee relations generally. But it is not part of Jewish economic doctrine and cannot be justified as a moral right or entitlement.[5]

It should be added that while the rabbis did not see the workplace as the venue for religious and personal fulfillment, they were also careful to insist that employees exhibit an almost religious commitment to the profits and the property of their employers. Nor would they allow undue piety to stand in the way of productivity. Even as employers were adjured to look upon their workers with compassion and understanding, workers were warned against waste and indolence on the job.

They also were enjoined from allowing off-hours activities, even those born of personal piety and godliness, from interfering with the energy and motivation that was an inherent expectation on the job. Further, despite the importance of ritual obligations, various prayers and blessings were curtailed or modified to accommodate the worker and the businessperson. This too was an easement for Jewish communities whose economic status was already precarious enough due to external pressures.

IV

Jewish sources are silent in yet another realm emerging from modern trends in organizational behavior. With some exceptions, the thrust of the Jewish ethical impulse is highly individualist. It speaks to a complex of obligations and norms that bind people to one other, to their communities, to their history, and to the Jewish nation. For our purposes, this means that responsibility resides in both the worker and the employer to fulfill the demands of their roles, with public authority mandated to correct their behavior in the breach. Accountability for sin and virtue, innocence and guilt are apportioned individually, with behavior rather than intent as the primary measure of morality. For the most part, penalties against wrongdoing are meted out in proportion to direct participation and involvement in the crime, and both penitence and restitution are highly personal.

In many areas of organizational behavior, such an ethic remains appropriate and efficacious. We have been treated to countless instances of wrongdoing perpetrated for the sole benefit of one or a small group of managers, directors, or investors, the corporate veil notwithstanding. In such cases there is little ambiguity in the behavior or the intent, the actions were clearly premeditated, and the victims, whether investors, clients, or local residents, are easily identified.

Consequently assigning accountability or guilt on an individual basis poses no difficulty. Traditional ethical categories stand well.

However, the continued collectivization of social and economic life has introduced another form of crime and wrongdoing for which these categories may be inadequate. We have long assumed that evil will be unambiguous, fitting preconceived notions about its genesis with the violence and direct injury it causes to innocent others. Moreover, we also have presupposed that those who are its perpetrators will be recognizable both in their own appearance and in their proximity to the act itself. As in old-fashioned western movies, villains were quickly identifiable by their dress, their speech, their actions, and the color of their horses.

In recent decades, however, we have been introduced to ambiguous and almost indistinguishable forms of evil resident in the corporate structures of business, government, and even charitable organizations. No longer composed of the violence and brutality that makes us recoil in its presence, such actions are less often wrought by knives and guns than by laptop computers and 57.6K bps modems. Moreover, the perpetrators may be well-meaning, even righteous individuals who look neither like monsters nor devils but more like clerks and neighbors. Buried deep within or atop bureaucratic structures in every sector of the economy, they rarely confront evil directly and easily purge themselves of responsibility for the deed, if they even define it as a crime. Upstanding and honorable in their private lives, they blanch from the mere thought of participation in behavior that may be defined as criminal or immoral.

It was this phenomenon that Hannah Arendt termed the "banality of evil" in her controversial diary of the Nazi war

crimes trial of Adolf Eichmann.[6] Most assuredly, it was superficial and naive for her to accept Eichmann's claim that he was
"just following orders," as much victim as perpetrator, a mere
cog in some large bureaucratic machine. Still, her observations
and their implication for employees of large corporate structures deserve fuller consideration, some forty years later. If
validated, they beg an alternative model of human behavior to
help structure a moral order and assign accountability not in
place of, but in addition to, the highly personal one we have
ascribed to classical Jewish thought.

In simplest terms, Arendt posited that in complex organizations, those in league with the devil no longer spit fire or carry
pitchforks. Rather, they wear white collars and sit at
mahogany desks several steps removed from the field of
action. They easily find themselves guiltless, for they perform
no bloody deed and remain ignorant (often purposefully) of
those who do. Nor do they make any corporate decision on
their own. Others, equally distinguished, respectable, and
authoritative, accede to the proposition. To object would be
futile, accomplishing nothing but to risk and jeopardize one's
own personal and professional future. Here Arendt's work
finds confluence with what Irving Janis calls "groupthink."[7]

If this is true of the perpetrators or their unwitting accessories, so too is the act itself banal. Precisely because today the
computer or the standardized form can work theft or corruption, they may be less recognizable as such. In organizations
where functional roles are fragmented and redundant,
employees operate under what some call "bounded rationality" and others less kindly term "muddling through." Here
employees implement their tasks anonymously and indiffer-
ently, becoming accessories simply by pursuing their work
without thinking.[8]

Psychologists speak of the mad and deranged propensities resident within our minds as psychopathic when they become an unthinking part of one's personal routine, so that one can no longer distinguish them from the normal. "Bureaupathic" behavior denotes similar tendencies within the organization. These dangerous irrationalities promote actions that individuals would never consider on their own, but by the force of organizational routine, soon become standard procedure. Evil may result from neglect and indifference as easily as from intent and design.[9]

We may add that the problem is exacerbated when the enterprise has a religious or nationalist mission. Precisely that which should motivate higher levels of integrity becomes a rationale for corruption in the name of the faith, the homeland, or the community of believers. Protected now by a veil of gnostic secrecy, even the Divine Will may be invoked as normally good, honest, and sincere individuals are moved to take actions they would never consider for personal gain.

Perhaps it may be added that the silence of Jewish sources here belies considerations that go beyond the recent vintage of such ruminations. Current organizational theorists and students of bureaucracy have taken Arendt to task for an evaluation of collective evil that is too facile even in its routine, indeed banal manifestations. From "whistleblowing" to the "democratic workplace " to stakeholder surveys, they demand individual accountability from all employees whether in the executive suite or on the front-line.

At the risk of reading too much into the classics, the silence of their contemporary interpreters on this phenomenon may suggest that for Jewish tradition, responsibility remains personal even in environs that are corporate by definition. As a just society is little more than a conglomeration of citizens in

pursuit of righteousness, so too an ethical corporation is little
more than a framework for the components that comprise it.
Difficult and foreboding as it may seem, to allow membership
in this collective to become a pretext for avoiding culpability is
to flirt with moral anarchy. When everyone stands responsible
for evil, then no one will be held accountable.[10]

V

Finally, let us admit to another and parallel motivation for
undertaking a study of this nature. In recent years Jewish
learning, as reflected in the writings of scholars and the interests of the laity, has progressively narrowed its scope. Large
portions of Jewish text have lain dormant, reserved, in the
main, for a handful of academic scholars and practitioners
generally apart from both the mainstream of Jewish learning
and the developing culture of the business community. In contrast, most adherents of the tradition have immersed themselves in religious studies that largely defined their relationship with the Almighty through the celebration of holy days,
life-cycle events, prayer, and ritual.

This is not to say that the commercial and civil aspects of
Jewish learning were always ignored. Ironically, they have
been central to the primary-school curriculum for centuries.
Most every schoolboy began his talmudic education with laws
pertaining to business relationships, torts, judicial procedure
in civil cases, and the purchase of real property. Nevertheless,
these studies remained largely academic and theoretical in
favor of the myriad detail and nuance in which ritual observance has become enwrapped. When a young man reached his
majority and stood to be ordained for religious and communal
leadership, it was his knowledge of dietary practices and holi-

day ritual that generally served as the core of his comprehensive examinations.

This disproportionate emphasis upon the ecclesiastical at the expense of the civil carries several important social implications. In the first place, it means that sanctity and righteousness are increasingly, though by no means universally, defined by expertise in and rigid observance of Jewish ritual. This phenomenon has a reinforcing and self-fulfilling quality, for the greater emphasis upon ritual produces religious virtuosi who are held aloft as models of piety. Moreover, those charged with monitoring religious behavior continue to exhort their students and congregants to increase their own stringency and demand that those around them conform to higher levels of religious behavior.

As a result, the gap between those within and those beyond the community of believers grows ever more distant and unbridgeable. For the committed, the prayers, holidays, and celebrations serve as the most evident public manifestations of faith, providing entrée to its confines, and a first bar to membership. However, for those on the fringes of this community and beyond, such observances are esoteric, anachronistic, and even bizarre. The common language or set of memories and values that might have forestalled mutual alienation has long since been pulled threadbare as these two poles of Jewish belonging are driven further apart.

Equally significant and more disturbing, emphasis on the ritual over the civil has provided believers with a dangerously mistaken impression. Though hardly justified by the tradition or by the lives of those who were its interpreters, it has been taken to imply that ethical values and behavior in business, interpersonal relations, or communal leadership are of lesser import than proper ritual behavior. It is difficult to ascertain whether this is a genuine misapprehension or little more than an excuse for misbehavior.

Yet, all the same, the results have often been scandalous. In the recent past, Jewish clerics in Israel and the Diaspora, alongside distinguished members of their congregations, all exhibiting the outward appearances associated with their faith, have been found guilty of various types of criminal behavior. Often preying on the most vulnerable members of their own communities, these crimes have generally been rooted in business or professional pursuits and related to interpersonal morality. Indeed, they were sometimes committed for the benefit of institutions of religious higher education and houses of prayer. This indifference to social ethics and its legal ramifications is compartmentalized from religious ritual. Evidence of righteousness and divine grace falls largely on the side of the latter.

The interested and often cynical outsider peering in at such doings takes these to confirm a harsh and unfair inference that he has always harbored. Those very individuals who preach godliness via prayer and study appear hypocritically bereft of the qualities that stand universal to all faith: honesty, integrity, and propriety in social interactions, perhaps most notably those that impinge upon business and professional trust. What can be the value of a faith that creates adherents with such lopsided sensibilities? Might it be that the tradition itself lacks an economic or social ethic? Minimally, the gap between themselves and the community of believers becomes even wider.

An attempt to correct this imbalance may have a twofold effect in promoting social healing. It will help believers return to the basic elements of morality manifested in interpersonal relations, elements that have always been inherent in the tradition and essential to piety and righteousness. This, of course, must be made manifest by behavior and practice. Yet emphasizing it in educational forums, from the curriculum to the sermon to popular literature, will signal its importance and centrality to those within, and equally important to those beyond, the bounds of the faith.

Additionally, attempts to hone and refine the presentation of these values in the form of codes of ethics and statements of trust will further trumpet their import. Might we consider a "Ten Commandments" of consumer protection, of employee rights and responsibilities, or of a commitment to value? Based on Jewish sources and text but written in a practical and accessible manner, this will showcase the richness of the tradition even as it will stand to promote the needs of the client and protect the honest employee or entrepreneur.

Equally, there is reason to believe that the study of business and professional ethics based in Jewish sources may have an unexpected value. Of course, the content itself has great significance as a source of Western culture. At the very least it is an available mound of untapped data for both religious and secular Jewish scholars and intellectuals.

However, there also may be something in studying this material to help bridge the gap between these two poles. The world of outreach has become an increasing part of activist Jewish organizations. Here the emphasis once again is upon prayer, ritual, and holiday observance, an effective mechanism for some of those so engaged. However, for many others it is yet one more attempt to missionize by persons of questionable credibility.

Moreover, the two groups, the unaffiliated and those reaching out to them, do not meet as equals. The former hold a lower status, owing to their distance from the topics and practices that form the core of their studies. They are, as the

Talmud would have it, "babes raised among the heathens." Their mentors are adjured, both by Jewish tradition and simple good sense, to treat them with tolerance and understanding. Yet there is little question that their ways hold no legitimacy and are fraught with ignorance or worse. The relationship is largely one-sided, save for the financial contributions that these neophytes might be called upon to provide.

By consequence, though they may be decades their junior, those providing the instruction tend to patronize their students, treating them in a childlike manner befitting the primary education for which this plan of study and their own training were originally developed. Precisely because one side is bereft of any preparation in this realm, they require intermediaries and cannot grapple as equals with the text or with the problems it confronts.

To be sure, it is unlikely that any of this is intentional. Further, it may be of marginal importance to a substantial portion of those who seek out and pursue a path of reconciliation with the traditions of their people. Yet it has a fatal effect on the interests of many others. And little will be done to accommodate their dissonance, for it is too often expressed only in their reticence to attend any such future encounters.

There might be value in shifting the course of outreach programming and study, at least for those to whom this "Hebrew school" approach has proven unsuccessful, toward a more sophisticated yet practical study of ethics and values. And what has more practical value than the financial and economic arena of life? Along with related areas of professional concern, this is a familiar subject for most people. They approach it with a sense of confidence borne of years of advanced education and professional practice. They can approach the text and the norms it represents from the standpoint of the world from which they stem. In brief, they can be treated as intelligent, thoughtful, reflective adults. Even if they are not moved to radically alter their life-style in its favor, they will have been engaged as adults, treated with dignity and respect, and will have devoted time to the study of Torah.

Of course that will require a substantial redirection for professionals in the Jewish community who see outreach to the unaffiliated as their primary calling. It will also demand profound changes in the training and education they receive and at the institutions that support them, including schools of rabbinic education. From business practices to biomedical ethics, from public policy toward the needy to social services for the elderly or for families in crisis, the total agenda of social and public concerns is fair game for this study. Those who propose to reach out will need to be expert in at least some of these areas, in the relevant Jewish texts, and in the application of one to the other. It will be hard work, a labor that can only succeed "by the sweat of your brow."

1. See e.g. Jacques Barzun, *From Dawn to Decadence* (NY: HarperCollins, 2000); Jennifer R. Morse, The Modern State as an Occasion of Sin" *Notre Dame Journal of Law* 11, no.2 (1997):531-548.

2. Gerald C.Treacy, *Rerum Novarum: The Condition of Labor* (NY: The Paulist Press, 1939); Michael Zigarelli, "Catholic Social Teaching and the Employment Relationship" *Journal of Business Ethics* 12 no.1 (1993) pp. 75-82; Michael Naughton and Gene R. Laczniak, "A Theological Context of Work from the Catholic Social Encyclical Tradition" *Journal of Business Ethics* 12 no.12 (1993): 981-984.

3. Michael Naughton, "Participation in the Organization: An Ethical Analysis from the Papal Social Tradition" *Journal of Business Ethics* 14 no.11 (1995): 923-935; idem,*The Good Stewards*. (Lanham MD: University of American Press, 1992).

4. Richard Tawney, *Religion and the Rise of Capitalism* (New Brunswick, NJ: Transaction Books, 1998); Gideon J. Rossouw,

"Where Have All the Christians Gone" *Journal of Business Ethics,* 13 no. 7 (1994): pp. 557-571

5. See e.g. Ronald Green, "Centesimus Annus: A Critical Jewish Perspective" *Journal of Business Ethics* 12, no.12 (1993): pp. 945-954

6. Hannah Arendt, *Eichmann in Jerusalem: A Report on the Banality of Evil.* (NY: Viking, 1963); see also Bernard J. Bergen, *The Banality of Evil: Hannah Arendt and "The Final Solution,"* (Lanham, MD: Rowman and Littlefield, 1998); and Stephen Miller, "A Note On The Banality Of Evil," *The Wilson Quarterly;* 22, no.4 (1998):54-59

7. Irving Janis, *Groupthink: Psychological Studies of Policy Decisions and Fiascoes* (Boston: Houghton Miflin, 1982).

8. See e.g. Herbert Simon, *Models of Bounded Rationality: Empirically Grounded Economic Theory* (Cambridge, Mass: MIT Press, 1997); Charles Lindblom, "The Science of Muddling Through" *Public Administration Review,* 19, no.1 (1959) pp.79-88; idem, "Still Muddling, Not Quite Through" *Public Administration Review,* 39, no.6 (1979) pp.517-526.

9. See e.g. Edward J. Giblin, "Bureaupathology: The Denigration of Competence," *Human Resource Management,* 20, no. 4 (1981):22-26; and David K. Banner, "Of Paradigm Transformation and Organizational Effectiveness," *Leadership & Organization Development Journal,* 8, no. 2 (1987):17-29.

10. See e.g. Charles W. Anderson, "The Place of Principles in Policy Analysis" *American Political Science Review* 73, no. 2 (1979):711-723; B. Victor and C. Stephens, "An Ethical Weather Report: Assessing the Organization's Ethical Climate" *Organizational Dynamics* 18, no.2 (1989):pp. 50-62; William G. Scott and David K. Hart, "Administrative Crisis: The Neglect of Metaphysical Speculation," *Public Administration Review,* 33, no.5 (1973): pp.415-422; Dennis Thompson, "Moral Responsibility of Public Officials: The Problem of Many Hands" *American Political Science Review* 74, no.3 (1980): pp.905-916; Gregory Foster, "Law, Morality and the Public Servant" *Public Administration Review,* 41 no.1 (1981):pp. 29-34.

Bibliography

Allen, W. David. "The Moonlighting Decisions of Unmarried Men and Women: Family and Labor Market Influences." *Atlantic Economic Journal* 26, no. 2 (1998): 190–205.

Altman, John. "Toward a Stakeholder-Based Policy Process." *Policy Sciences* 27, no. 1 (1994): 37–51.

Anderson, Charles W. "The Place of Principles in Policy Analysis" *American Political Science Review* 73, no. 2 (1979):711-723.

Anthony, P. D. *The Ideology of Work.* London: Tavistock, 1977.

Arcuri, Alan, et al. "Moonlighting by Police Officers: A Way of Life." *Psychological Reports* 60, no. 2 (1987): 210–211.

Arendt, Hannah. *Eichmann in Jerusalem: A Report on the Banality of Evil.* New York: Viking, 1963.

Baba, Vishwanath, and Muhammad Jamal. "How Much Do We Really Know About Moonlighters?" *Public Personnel Management* 21, no. 1 (1992): 65–73.

Baird, Charles. "American Union Law: Source of Conflict." *Journal of Labor Research* 11, no. 3 (1990): 269–292.

———. "On Strikers and Their Replacements." *Government Union Review* 12, no. 3 (1991): 1–30.

Banner, David K. "Of Paradigm Transformation and Organizational Effectiveness." *Leadership & Organization Development Journal,* 8, no. 2 (1987):17-29.

Barenberg, Mark. "The Political Economy of the Wagner Act: Power, Symbol, and Workplace Cooperation." *Harvard Law Review* 106, no. 7 (1993): 1379–1496.

Baron, Salo. *The Russian Jew Under Czars and Soviets*. New York: Macmillan, 1976.

Barzun, Jacques. *From Dawn to Decadence* NY: HarperCollins, 2000.

Baumhart, Richard. *An Honest Profit: What Businessmen Say About Ethics in Business*. New York: Holt, Rinehart & Winston, 1991.

Bazak, Jacob. "Judicial Ethics in Jewish Law." *Jewish Law Association Studies* 3 (1987): 28–37.

Beauchamp, Tom, and Norman Bowie, eds., *Ethical Theory and Business*. Englewood Cliffs, N.J.: Prentice-Hall, 1988.

Bergen, Bernard J., *The Banality of Evil: Hannah Arendt and "The Final Solution."* Lanham, MD: Rowman and Littlefield, 1998.

Bernstein, Paul. *American Work Values: Their Origin and Development*. Albany: State University of New York Press, 1997.

Bleich, J. David. *Contemporary Halachic Problems*. New York: Yeshiva University Press, 1977.

———. *Contemporary Halachic Problems*, vol. II. New York: Yeshiva University Press, 1983.

Blumfield, Hanita. "Jewish Women Sew the Union Label." *Humanity and Society* 6, no. 1 (1982): 33–45.

Brams, Steven. *Biblical Games: A Strategic Analysis of Stories in the Old Testament*. Cambridge: MIT Press, 1980.

Braude, Leonard. *Work and Workers*. New York: Praeger, 1975.

Clarkson, Max. "A Stakeholder Framework for Analyzing and Evaluating Corporate Social Performance." *Academy of Management Review* 20, no. 1 (1995): 92–117.

Coates, Norman. "The 'Confucian Ethic' and the Spirit of Japanese Capitalism." *Leadership and Organizational Development Journal* 2, no. 3 (1987): 17–23.

Cohen, Arnold. *An Introduction to Jewish Civil Law*. Jerusalem: Feldheim, 1991.

Cohen, Stuart. *The Three Crowns: Structures of Communal Discourse in Early Rabbinic Society.* Cambridge: Cambridge University Press, 1990.

Cover, Robert. "Obligation: A Jewish Jurisprudence of the Social Order." *Journal of Law and Religion* 5 (1987): 65–90.

Culler, Steven, and Gloria Bazzoli. "The Moonlighting Decisions of Resident Physicians." *Journal of Health Economics* 4, no. 3 (1985): 283–292.

Cushmir, Leonard, and Christine Koberg. "Religion and Attitudes Toward Work: A New Look at an Old Question." *Journal of Organizational Behavior* 9, no. 4 (1988): 251–262.

Davidson, James, and David P. Cadell. "Religion and the Meaning of Work." *Journal for the Scientific Study of Religion* 33, no. 2 (1994): 135–142.

Davidson, Jeffrey. "Curtail Moonlighting with Solid Guidelines and Performance Evaluations." *Data Management* 24, no. 1 (1986): 26–27.

Dempster, Donna, and Phyllis Moen. "Moonlighting Husbands: A Life-Cycle Perspective." *Work and Occupations* 16, no. 2 (1989): 43–64.

Dilts, David. "Privatization of the Public Sector: De Facto Standardization of Labor Law." *Journal of Collective Negotiations in the Public Sector* 24, no. 1 (1995): 37–43.

Donaldson, Thomas, and Lee E. Preston. "The Stakeholder Theory of the Corporation: Concepts, Evidence and Implications." *Academy of Management Review* 20, no. 1 (1995): 65–91.

Dose, Jennifer. "Work Values: An Integrative Framework and Illustrative Application to Organizational Socialization." *Journal of Occupational and Organizational Psychology* 70, no. 3 (1997): 219–240

Dubin, Robert, and Amira Galin. "Attachments to Work: Russians in Israel." *Work and Occupations* 19, no. 2 (1991): 172–193.

Eisen, Robert. "'Lifnim MiShurat Ha-Din' in Maimonides' *Mishneh Torah.*" *Jewish Quarterly Review* 89, nos. 3–4 (1999): 291–317.

Elazar, Daniel. "The Kehillah: From Its Beginnings to the End of the Modern Epoch." In Sam Lehman-Wilzig and Bernard Susser, eds., *Comparative Jewish Politics: Public Life in Israel and the Diaspora.* Jerusalem: Bar-Ilan University Press, 1981.

———. *Kinship and Consent: The Jewish Political Tradition and Its Contemporary Uses.* Lanham, Md.: University Press of America, 1983.

———. *The Jewish Polity: Jewish Political Organization from Biblical Times to the Present.* Bloomington: Indiana University Press, 1985.

Elon, Menahem. *Ha-Mishpat Ha-Ivri:Toldotav, Mekorotav, Ikronotav* . Jerusalem: Hebrew University. 1978.

Evan, William, and R. Edward Freeman. "A Stakeholder Theory of the Modern Corporation: Kantian Economics," In Tom Beauchamp & Norman Bowie, eds. *Ethical Theory and Business* (Englewood Cliffs, NJ: Prentice Hall, 1988).

Robert Factor, ed., "Moonlighting: Why Training Programs Should Monitor Residents' Activities." *Hospital and Community Psychiatry* 42, no. 3 (1991): 738.

———. "What Residents Do in Their Free Time Is Their Decision." *Hospital and Community Psychiatry* 42, no. 3 (1991): 739–742.

Farh, Jing-Lih, et al. "The Influence of Relational Demography and Quanxi: The Chinese Case." *Organizational Science* 9, no. 4 (1998): 471–488.

Federbush, Simon. *The Jewish Concept of Labor.* New York: Torah Culture Department, Jewish Agency, 1956.

Feingold, Henry. *Zion in America.* New York: Hippocrene, 1974.

Feldstein, Stanley. *The Land That I Show You: Three Centuries of Jewish Life in America.* New York: Doubleday, 1978.

Findling, Rabbi Moshe. *Hukat Ha-Avodah.* Jerusalem: Schreiber, 1941.

Foster, Gregory. "Law, Morality and the Public Servant" *Public Administration Review,* 41, no.1 (1981): 29-34.

Fraser, Bruce. "The Moonlight Shines on White Collars." *Nation's Business* 71, no. 7 (1983): 52–53.

Freeman, R. Edward. *Strategic Management: A Stakeholder Approach.* Boston: Pitman, 1984.

———. "The Politics of Stakeholder Theory: Some Future Directions." *Business Ethics Quarterly* 4, no. 4 (1994): 409–421.

——— and William Evan. "Corporate Governance: A Stakeholder Interpretation." *Journal of Behavioral Economics* 19, no. 4 (1990): 337–359.

——— and D. R. Gilbert. "Managing Stakeholder Relationships." In S. P. Sethi and C. M. Falbe, eds., *Business and Society.* Lexington: Lexington Books, 1987.

——— and D. L. Reed. "Stockholders and Stakeholder: A New Perspective on Corporate Governance." *California Management Review* 25, no. 3 (1983): 88–106.

Friedell, Steven. "The Different Voice in Jewish Law: Some Parallels to a Feminist Jurisprudence." *Indiana Law Journal* 67 (1992): 915–949.

Friedman, H. H. "Ethical Behavior in Business: A Hierarchical Approach from the Talmud." *Journal of Business Ethics* 4, no. 2 (1985): 117–129.

Friedman, Milton. *Capitalism and Freedom.* Chicago: University of Chicago Press, 1962.

——. "The Social Responsibility of Business Is to Increase Its Profits." *New York Times Magazine,* September 13, 1970.

Furnham, Arthur. *The Protestant Work Ethic: The Psychology of Work Related Beliefs and Ethics.* London: Routledge, 1990.

—— and M. Rose. "Alternative Ethics: The Relationship Between the Wealth, Welfare, Work and Leisure Ethic." *Human Relations* 40, no. 3 (1987): 561–574.

—— et al. "A Comparison of Protestant Work Ethic Beliefs in Thirteen Nations." *Journal of Social Psychology* 133, no. 2 (1993): 185–197.

Giblin, Edward J. "Bureaupathology: The Denigration of Competence," *Human Resource Management,* 20, no. 4 (1981):22-26.

Goodpaster, Kenneth. "Business Ethics and Stakeholder Analysis." *Business Ethics Quarterly* 1 (1991): 61–70.

Greeley, Andrew. "The Protestant Ethic: Time for a Moratorium." *Sociological Analysis* 25, no. 3 (1964): 20–33.

Green, Ronald M. "Centesimus Annus: A Critical Jewish Perspective." *Journal of Business Ethics* 12, no. 12 (1993): 945–954.

Greenberg, Rabbi Mordecai. *Henaheg Bahem Minhag Derekh Eretz: Bayn Torah VeAvodah LeToratam Umnatam,* Yavneh:Yeshivat Kerem B'Yavneh, 1999.

"Ha-anakah" in Rabbi S.Y. Zevin (ed.) *Encyclopedia Talmudit* Jerusalem: Yad Harav Herzog, 1973: 9:774-787

Harpaz, Itzhak. *The Meaning of Work in Israel: Its Nature and Consequences.* New York: Praeger, 1990.

——. "A Cross National Comparison of Religious Conviction and the Meaning of Work." *Cross Cultural Research* 32, no. 2 (1998): 143–170.

———. "The Transformation of Work Values in Israel." *Monthly Labor Review* 122, no. 5 (1999): 46–51.

Herman, Robert, et al. *The Jossey-Bass Handbook of Non-Profit Leadership and Management.* San Francisco: Jossey-Bass, 1994.

Hertzberg, Arthur. *The Zionist Idea: A Historical Analysis and Reader.* New York: Atheneum, 1975.

"Hezkat Serarah" in Rabbi S.Y. Zevin (ed.) *Encyclopedia Talmudit,* Jerusalem: Rabbi Herzog Institute, 1973: 14:346-373.

Hofstede, G. "Motivation, Leadership and Organization: Do American Theories Apply Abroad?" *Organizational Dynamics* 9, no. 2 (1980): 42–63.

———. "The Cultural Relativity of Organizational Practices and Theories." *Journal of International Business Studies* 14, no. 2 (1983): 75–90.

———. *Culture and Organizations: Software of the Mind.* London: McGraw-Hill, 1991.

———. "Cultural Constraints on Management Theories." *Academy of Management Executive* 7, no. 2 (1993): 81–94.

Hopkins, Michael, and Jeffrey L. Seglin. "Americans@work." *Inc* 19, no. 5 (1997): 77–85.

Israel, Richard. "Supervision, Rabbinic Style: Some Texts and Commentary." *Journal of Jewish Communal Service* 64, no. 2 (1987): 141–144.

Jamal, Muhammad. "Moonlighting: Personal, Social and Organizational Consequences." *Human Relations* 39, no. 3 (1986): 977–990.

———. Is Moonlighting Mired in Myth? *Personnel Journal* 67, no. 2 (1988): 48–53.

——— and Ronald Crawford. "Consequences of Extended Work Hours: A Comparison of Moonlighters, Overtimers and Modal Employees." *Human Resources Management* 20, no. 3 (1981): 18–23.

Janis, Irving. *Groupthink: Psychological Studies of Policy Decisions and Fiascoes* Boston: Houghton Miflin, 1982.

Jones, Thomas M. "Instrumental Stakeholder Theory: A Synthesis of Ethics and Economics." *Academy of Management Review* 20, no. 2 (1995): 404–437.

―――― et al. "The Toronto Conference: Reflections on Stakeholder Theory." *Business and Society* 33, no. 1 (1994): 82–131.

Joslit, Jenna W. "Saving Souls: The Vocational Training of American Jewish Women, 1880-1930" in *An Inventory of Promises: Essays in Honor of Moses Rischin*, ed. Jeffrey S. Gurock and Marc Lee Raphael, 151-169. Brooklyn: Carlson, 1995.

Katz, Mordecai. *Protection of the Weak in the Talmud*. New York: Columbia University Press, 1925.

Keely, John, and James Ryan. "Should Police Moonlight in Security Jobs?" *Security Management* 27, no. 3 (1983): 9–18.

Kimmel, Jean, and Lisa M. Powell. "Moonlighting Trends and Related Policy Issues in Canada and the United States." *Canadian Public Policy* 25, no. 2 (1999): 207–231.

Klinger, Donald. "Public Sector Bargaining." *Review of Public Personnel Administration* 13, no. 3 (1993): 19–28.

Koeller, Timothy. "Union Activity and the Decline in American Trade Union Membership." *Journal of Labor Research* 15, no. 1 (1994): 19–32.

Langtry, Bruce. "Stakeholders and the Moral Responsibility of Business." *Business Ethics Quarterly* 4, no. 4 (1994): 431–443.

LaPlante, Alice. "Outside Work OK If You Ask." *Computerworld* 25, no. 12 (1991): 101.

Lenski, Gerhard. *The Religious Factor*. Garden City, N.Y.: Doubleday, 1963.

Leonard, Bill . "Rate of Moonlighting Among Workers Holds a Steady Pace." *Human Resources Magazine* 42, no. 7 (1997): 10.

Levi, Yehuda. *Torah Study: A Survey of Classic Sources on Timely Issues.* Jerusalem: Feldheim, 1990.

Levin, Nora. *While Messiah Tarried: Jewish Socialist Movements, 1871–1917.* New York: Schocken, 1977.

Levine, Aaron. *Economics and Jewish Law.* New York: Ktav, 1980.

———. *Free Enterprise and Jewish Law.* New York: Yeshiva University Press, 1987.

——— and Moses Pava, eds. *Jewish Business Ethics: The Firm and Its Stakeholders.* Northvale, N.J.: Jason Aronson, 1999.

Levy, Charles S. "Occupational Values and Ethics in Jewish Law and Lore: Premises for Jewish Communal Service." *Journal of Jewish Communal Service* 52, no. 1 (1976) 133–140.

Lincoln, James, and Arne Kalleberg. "Work and Work Force Commitment: A Study of Plants and Employment in the US and Japan." *Sociological Review* 30, no. 1 (1985): 738–760.

Lindblom, Charles. "The Science of Muddling Through" *Public Administration Review,* 19, no.1 (1959): 79-88.

_____ "Still Muddling, Not Quite Through" *Public Administration Review,* 39, no.6 (1979): 517-526.

Lipset, Seymour Martin. "The Work Ethic, Then and Now." *Public Interest* 35, no. 4 (1990): 61–69.

Little, Charles. "Sociological Moonlighting: Practical Advice About Consulting for Local Government." *Sociological Practice Review* 2, no. 3 (1991): 217–223.

Markowitz, Ruth J. *My Daughter, the Teacher: Jewish Teachers in the New York City School System.* New York: Ktav, 1981.

Mannheim, Bilha, and Avraham Sella. "Work Values in the Oral Torah." *Journal of Psychology and Judaism* 15, no. 4 (1991): 241–260.

May, Cathy. "Moonlighting: It's a Question of DP Ethics." *Data Management* 23, no. 3 (1985): 10.

McClelland, David. *The Achieving Society.* Princeton, N.J.: Van Nostrand, 1961.

McGammon, Holly. "Legal Limits on Labor Militancy: Labor Law and the Right to Strike Since the New Deal." *Social Problems* 37, no. 2 (1990): 206–229.

———. "Government by Injunction: The US Judiciary and Strike Action in the Late 19th and Early 20th Centuries." *Work and Occupations* 20, no. 2 (1993): 174–204.

———. "From Repressive Intervention to Integrative Prevention: The US State's Legal Management of Labor Militancy." *Social Forces* 71, no. 3 (1993): 569–601.

Miller, Stephen. "A Note On The Banality Of Evil," *The Wilson Quarterly;* 22, no.4 (1998):54-59.

"Moonlighting for Moola." *American Demographics* 19, no. 3 (1997): 41.

Morse, Jennifer R. "The Modern State as an Occasion of Sin" *Notre Dame Journal of Law* 11, no.2 (1997):531-548.

MOW International Research Team. *The Meaning of Work.* London: Academic Press, 1987

"Multiple Jobholders by Selected Demographic and Economic Characteristics." *Employment and Earnings* 6, no. 2 (1999): 67.

"Multiple Jobholding Reached Record High in May." *Bureau of Labor Statistics News,* 89-529 (1989): 1–5.

Naughton, Michael. "Participation in the Organization: An Ethical Analysis from the Papal Social Tradition" *Journal of Business Ethics* 14, no.11 (1995): 923-935.

—————*The Good Stewards.* Lanham MD: University of American Press, 1992.

————— and Gene R. Laczniak. "A Theological Context of Work from the Catholic Social Encyclical Tradition" *Journal of Business Ethics* 12, no.12 (1993): 981-984.

Nelson, Margaret K. "Between Paid and Unpaid Work: Gender Patterns in Supplemental Economic Activities Among White Rural Families." *Gender and Society;* 13, no. 4 (1999): 518–539.

Neu, Irene D. "The Jewish Business Woman In America" American *Jewish Historical Quarterly* 66, no.1 (1976): 137-154;

Niles, F. S. "Toward a Cross Cultural Understanding of Work Related Beliefs." *Human Relations* 52, no. 7 (1999): 855–867.

Osigweh, C. A. B. "Elements of an Employee Rights and Responsibilities Paradigm." *Journal of Management* 16, no. 4 (1990): 835–850.

———. "Toward an Employee Rights and Responsibilities Paradigm." *Human Relations* 43, 12 (1991): 1277–1309.

———. "A Stakeholder Perspective of Employee Responsibilities and Rights." *Employee Responsibilities and Rights Journal* 7, no. 4 (1994): 279–296.

Pawlak, Edward, and June Bays. "Executive Perspectives on Part-Time Private Practice." *Administration in Social Work* 12, no. 1 (1988): 1–11.

Pava, Moses. *Business Ethics: A Jewish Perspective.* New York: Yeshiva University Press, 1997.

———. *Ethics and Legality in Jewish Law.* Jerusalem: Amiel Library, 1997.

Peled, Lisa Hope, and Katherine Xin. "Work Values and Their Human Resource Management Implications: A Theoretical Comparison of China, Mexico and the United States." *Journal of Applied Management Studies* 6, no. 2 (1997): 185–198.

Perry, Michael. *Labor Rights in the Jewish Tradition.* Jewish Labor Committee, n.d.

Pipkin, R. M. "Moonlighting in Law School." *American Bar Association Research Journal* (1982): 1109–1162.

Posner, B. Z., and William H. Schmidt. "Values and the American Manager." *California Management Review* 26, no. 3 (1984): 202–216.

Preston, Lee, and H. J. Sapeinza. "Stakeholder Management and Corporate Performance." *Journal of Behavioral Economics* 19, no. 4 (1990): 361–375.

Preston, Richard. *The Future of Christian Ethics*. London: SCM Press, 1987.

Raffel, Jeffrey, and Lance Groff . "Shedding Light on the Dark Side of Teacher Moonlighting." *Educational Evaluation and Policy Analysis* 12, no. 4 (1990): 403–414.

Ralston, David A. "The Impact of National Culture and Economic Ideology on Managerial Work Values: A Study of the United States, Russia, Japan and China." *Journal of International Business Studies* 28, no. 1 (1997): 177–208.

———. "Doing Business in the 21st Century with the New Generation of Chinese Managers: A Study of Generational Shifts in Work Values in China." *Journal of International Business Studies* 30, no. 2 (1999): 415–428.

Reineke, Robert A. "Stakeholder Involvement in Evaluation: Suggestions for Practice." *Evaluation Practice* 12, no. 1 (1991): 39–44.

Rose, Michael. *Reworking the Work Ethic: Economic Values and Socio-Cultural Politics*. London: Schocken, 1985.

Rossouw, Gideon J. "Where Have All the Christians Gone?" *Journal of Business Ethics* 13, no. 7 (1994): 557–571.

Sachar, Howard. *The Course of Modern Jewish History*. New York: Delta, 1976.

Santangelo, Sole, and David Lester. "Correlates of Job Satisfaction of Public School Teachers: Moonlighting, Locus of Control and Stress." *Psychological Reports* 58, no. 1 (1985): 130.

Schappes, Morris. "The Political Origins of the Hebrew Trades." *Journal of Ethnic Studies* 5, no. 1 (1977): 13–44.

Schor, Philip. "Public Service as a Calling: An Exploration of a Concept, Part II." *International Journal of Public Administration* 13, no. 5 (1990): 649–691.

Schreiber, Aaron. *Jewish Law and Decision-Making: A Study Through Time.* Philadelphia: Temple University Press, 1979.

Scott, William G. and David K. Hart. "Administrative Crisis: The Neglect of Metaphysical Speculation," *Public Administration Review,* 33, no.5 (1973): 415-422.

Shamir, B. "Protestant Work Ethic, Work Involvement and the Psychological Impact of Unemployment." *Journal of Occupational Behavior* 7, no. 2 (1986): 25–38.

Shepard, J. C. *The Law of Fiduciaries.* Toronto: Carswell, 1981.

Shilo, Shmuel. "One Aspect of Law and Morals in Jewish Law: 'Lifnim Meshurat Hadin.'" *Israel Law Review* 13 (1978): 359–390.

Simon, Herbert. *Models of Bounded Rationality: Empirically Grounded Economic Theory.* Cambridge, Mass: MIT Press, 1997.

Sloan, Allan. "For Whom the Bell Tolls." *Newsweek,* January 15, 1996, p. 37.

Snow, Carlton J., and Elliott M. Abramson. "By the Light of Dual Employment: Standards for Employer Regulation of Moonlighting." *Indiana Law Journal* 55, no. 4 (1980): 581–614.

Steinberg, Abraham, and Fred Rosner. "Sources of the Debate: Torah Alone or Torah Together with Worldly Occupation." *Journal of Halacha and Contemporary Society* 32, no. 3 (1996): 65–93.

Stinson, John. "Moonlighting by Women Jumped to Record Highs." *Monthly Labor Review* 109, no. 11 (1986): 22–25.

———. "Moonlighting: A Key to Differences in Employment Growth." *Monthly Labor Review* 110, no. 2 (1987): 30–31.

————. "Multiple Jobholding Up Sharply in the 1980's." *Monthly Labor Review* 113, no. 7 (1990): 3–10.

————. "New Data on Multiple Jobholding Available from the CPS." *Monthly Labor Review* 120, no. 3 (1997): 3–8.

Stone, Suzanne. "In Pursuit of the Counter Text: The Turn to the Jewish Legal Model in Contemporary American Legal Theory." *Harvard Law Review* 106 (1993): 813–894.

Tamari, Meir. *With All Your Possessions: Jewish Ethics and Economic Life.* New York: Free Press, 1987.

————. "Ethical Issues in Bankruptcy: A Jewish Perspective." *Journal of Business Ethics* 9, no. 10 (1990): 785–789.

————. *In the Marketplace: Jewish Business Ethics.* Jerusalem: Targum/Feldheim, 1991.

————. "The Social Responsibilities of the Jewish Individual." In David Schatz et al., eds., *Tikun Olam: Social Responsibility in Jewish Thought.* Northvale, N.J.: Jason Aronson, 1997.

Tawney, Richard. *Religion and the Rise of Capitalism.* New Brunswick, NJ: Transaction Books, 1998.

Taylor M. H., and A. E. Filmer. "Moonlighting: The Practical Problems." *Canadian Public Administration* 29, no. 3 (1997): 592–597.

Thompson, Dennis. "Moral Responsibility of Public Officials: The Problem of Many Hands" *American Political Science Review* 74, no.3 (1980): 905-916.

Tilgher, Arthur. *Homo Faber: Work Through the Ages.* New York: Harcourt Brace, 1930.

Treacy, Gerald C. *Rerum Novarum: The Condition of Labor.* New York: The Paulist Press, 1939.

Upton, Richard. "Moonlighting: A Dark Shadow on the White Economy." *Personnel Management* 12, no. 2 (1980): 28–31.

Victor B. and C. Stephens, "An Ethical Weather Report: Assessing the Organization's Ethical Climate" *Organizational Dynamics* 18, no.2 (1989): 50-62.

Waddell, Bill. "Authorized Moonlighting." *Business Forum* 15, no. 1 (1983): 32.

Wagschal, S. *Torah Guide for the Businessman.* Spring Valley, N.Y.: Feldheim, 1990.

Wahrhaftig, Shillem. *Dinei Avodah Be-Mishpat Ivrei* (1969). Tel Aviv: Moreshet. 2 Vol.

Wallace, Michael, et al. "American Labor Law: Its Impact on Working Class Militancy." *Social Science History* 12, no. 1 (1988): 1–29.

Walzer, Michael. *Exodus and Revolution.* New York: Basic Books, 1986.

Weber, Max. *The Protestant Ethic and the Spirit of Capitalism.* New York: Scribner's, 1958.

Weisfeld, Israel. *Labor Legislation in the Bible and Talmud.* New York: Yeshiva University Press, 1974.

Whitley, James. "Moonlighting: A Good Educational Experience for Residents." *Investigative Radiology* 22, no. 3 (1987): 693.

Wicks, Andrew, et al. "A Feminist Reinterpretation of the Stakeholder Concept." *Business Ethics Quarterly* 4, no. 4 (1994): 475–497.

Wildavsky, Aaron. *The Nursing Father: Moses as Political Leader.* Tuscaloosa: University of Alabama Press, 1984.

———. *Assimilation vs. Separation: Joseph the Administrator and the Politics of Religion in Biblical Israel.* New Brunswick, N.J.: Transaction Books, 1992.

Williamson, Oscar. *The Law of Discretionary Behavior.* London: Kershaw, 1965.

Wisniewski, Robert, and Paul Kliene. "Teacher Moonlighting: An Unstudied Phenomenon." *Phi Delta Kappan* 65, no. 3 (1984): 553–55.

Wolkinson, Benjamin. "Labor and the Jewish Tradition—A

Reappraisal." *Jewish Social Studies* 40, nos. 3–4 (1977): 231–238.

Worthy, J. C. *Shaping an American Institution: Robert E. Wood and Sears, Roebuck.* Urbana: University of Illinois, 1984.

Zigarelli, Michael. "Catholic Social Teaching and the Employment Relationship" *Journal of Business Ethics* 12, no.1 (1993): 75-82.

Index

Freedom *vs.* obligation, Rights
  vs. responsibility, 7
Freeman, R. Edward, 105
Friedman, Milton, 103–104

G

Gamliel, Rabban, 77
Garmu, House of, 154–156
General Electric Corporation,
  104
Germany, work values of, and
  religious convictions, 63
God's elect or chosen, 42
Gompers, Samuel, 147
Goodpaster, Kenneth, 121
Gordon, A.D., 148
Greece, classical, ideals of, 61
"Greek wisdom," 76
"Groupthink," 199
Guanxi (social connections and
  indebtedness), 45
Guild, 152. *See also* Organized
  labor

H

Ha-anakah (gratuity or bonus to
  indentured Hebrew), 111
ha-Golah, Rabbi Gershom
  Me'or, 134, 140
ha-Kohen, Rabbi Yisrael Meir,
  88, 89, 90
ha-Turim, Rabbi Yaakov ben
  Asher Ba'al, 52, 85
Halevi, Rabbi Mordechai, 84
Hanina, Rabbi, 57–58

Hanna, Rabbah bar (bar Hanan,
  bar Rav Huna), 24–25, 26–27
Haredi community, 69–70,
  99–100
Health-care providers, striking
  by, 159
Heaven, fear of, 49–50, 60
Hebrew servant, 20, 21. *See also*
  Indentured servant
High-risk occupations, 27
Hillel, Rabbi Mordecai ben, 20,
  132
Histadrut, 148
History, Jewish
  overview, 5–7
  pre-modern communities,
    82–83
  of public sector employees,
    167–169
Hofstede's cultural taxonomy of
  the work ethic, 43–44, 62
Holiness, and employment in
  the public sector, 170–171, 181,
  182
Holland, work values of, and
  religious convictions, 63

I

Idleness. *See* Productivity
Imbalance in social relation-
  ships, 16
Indentured servant, 18–22, 36,
  111–112, 115
Indifference, and neglect, mod-
  ern evil of, 200
Individual growth, 2–3, 189, 196
Injuries, work-related, 116

About the Author

David J. Schnall is Dean of the Azrieli Graduate School of Jewish Education and Herbert Schiff Chair in Management and Administration at the Wurzweiler School of Social Work of Yeshiva University. During 1999–2000, he served as J. William Fulbright Visiting Professor and Senior Scholar at the Baerwald School of Social Work of the Hebrew University in Jerusalem. He has taught at Long Island University, the City University of New York, and Fordham University, and served as Visiting Scholar at the Hastings Center for Ethics.

Professor Schnall was ordained at the Rabbi Isaac Elchanan Theological Seminary and he holds a Ph.D. in political science from Fordham University. He is a well-known author and lecturer in such diverse areas as Jewish affairs, Mid-East politics, American public policy, and organizational management in the tax exempt sector. His previous books include *Beyond the Green Line: Israeli Settlements West of the Jordan, Contemporary Issues in Health Care, The Jewish Agenda, Ethnicity and Suburban Local Politics,* and *Cracks in the Wall: Radical Dissent in Contemporary Israeli Politics.* He is also co-editor of *Crisis and Continuity: The Jewish Family Faces the 21st Century,* and *A Portrait of the American Jewish Community,* and co-developer of the *SingWin®* evaluation and instructional software system.

An active consultant in planning and human resource development, Dr. Schnall's client list includes local government agencies, major medical centers, and Jewish charitable, educational and communal organizations in New York and Jerusalem. His columns appear regularly in the Jewish and general media and he is listed in *Who's Who In America*. He lives on Long Island with his wife Tova and their three children, Eliezer, Etan and Yonina.